ETHNICITY AND NATIONALISM

Anthrop

D0370569

Anthropology, Culture and Society

Series Editor: Dr Richard Wilson, University of Essex

Anthropological Perspectives on Politics:
The Comparative Study of Power in Society
JOHN GLEDHILL

Anthropology and Development
KATY GARDNER

Economic Anthropology
SUSANA NAROTZKY

ETHNICITY
AND
NATIONALISM

Anthropological Perspectives

Thomas Hylland Eriksen

Pluto Press

LONDON • BOULDER, COLORADO

First published by Pluto Press
345 Archway Road, London N6 5AA
and 5500 Central Avenue,
Boulder, Colorado 80301, USA

94 96 98 97 95
2 4 6 5 3

© 1993 Thomas Hylland Eriksen

The right of Thomas Hylland Eriksen to be identified
as author of this work has been asserted by him
in accordance with the Copyright, Designs and Patents Act, 1988.

ISBN 0 7453 0700 0 hbk
ISBN 0 7453 0701 9 pbk

Printed in Finland by WSOY

CONTENTS

SERIES EDITOR'S PREFACE

This is the first book in the new Pluto Press anthropology series, which aims to introduce a wide audience to anthropological thinking on a variety of themes; including kinship, politics, sexuality, rationality, development, medical anthropology and economics.

In this series, leading scholars present, in an accessible form, the state of the debate in their field, and advance their own views and insights. The editorial policy explicitly encourages contributions from a range of theoretical perspectives.

It is appropriate that this series begins with the theme of identity, one of the most pressing issues of the day. As ethnicity and nationalism take on a new political significance, it is important to reflect critically on the implications of the politics of identity. Eriksen makes the case well for what anthropology has to offer to the understanding of social classification processes.

Anthropology has developed many of the more nuanced and complex insights into symbolism and meaning, which is the substance of identity. Ethnography, the primary research method of anthropology, is one of the best ways of understanding peoples' subjective perceptions of historical processes. Through ethnography, one can understand issues of world importance through the everyday practices and values of ordinary people. As Eriksen points out, this is exactly where ethnicity is created and recreated. Finally, anthropology's approach is cross-cultural, which is a powerful tool for showing how the seemingly natural categories of nations and ethnic groups are historical, contextual and socially constructed.

Eriksen is to be commended for his thorough and comprehensive survey of anthropological contributions to the study of social classification processes. In addition, he adds to theoretical debate, considering the implications of gender, theories of post-modernity and globalisation for the understanding of ethnic and national identities.

Dr Richard Wilson
Series Editor

PREFACE

This book was written thanks to an invitation from Richard Wilson and Pluto Press. Upon receiving the invitation, I believed I would not have the time to undertake the task. Having reflected on the matter, I quickly realised I would be unable not to. I have not regretted this decision: it has been a pleasure to work on this book, which deals with a topic about which I feel great enthusiasm.

The study of ethnicity and nationalism forms the empirical focus of much contemporary anthropological research, and it has also been instrumental in raising theoretical and methodological issues of great importance, as well as providing models for understanding the contemporary world. Ethnic relations can be identified in virtually every society in the world and, contrary to much popular opinion, they may just as well be balanced and peaceful as they may be violent and volatile. Social anthropology is unique among the social sciences in offering a variety of research methods to investigate these phenomena, while simultaneously providing theoretical concepts and models that enable us to understand, account for and compare diverse ethnic phenomena.

Several people have been involved – wittingly or unwittingly – in the process of writing this book. Richard Wilson and Leif John Fosse have both read the entire manuscript critically, and their comments have been enlightening and very useful. Several of my colleagues and students have commented on ideas and concepts, especially concerning the relationship of ethnicity to gender and class. My former teachers at the Department and Museum of Anthropology, University of Oslo – Eduardo Archetti, Harald Eidheim and Axel Sommerfelt – should also be acknowledged for having taught me, among other things, that ethnicity is not self-explanatory. Finally, a nod of recognition must be directed towards the people who invented word processing, which enables authors to remain in total command of their own work until it is completed.

Oslo, June 1993

1 WHAT IS ETHNICITY?

It takes at least two somethings to create a difference ... Clearly each alone is – for the mind and perception – a non-entity, a non-being. Not different from being, and not different from non-being. An unknowable, a *Ding an sich*, a sound from one hand clapping.

Gregory Bateson (1979: 78)

Words like 'ethnic groups', 'ethnicity' and 'ethnic conflict' have become quite common terms in the English language, and they keep cropping up in the press, in TV news, in political programmes and in casual conversations. The same can be said for 'nation' and 'nationalism', and many of us have to admit that the meaning of these terms frequently seems ambiguous and vague.

There has been a parallel development in the social sciences. During the 1980s and early 1990s, we have witnessed an explosion in the growth of scholarly publications on ethnicity and nationalism, particularly in the fields of political science, history, sociology and social anthropology.

In the case of social anthropology, ethnicity has been a main preoccupation since the late 1960s and it remains a central focus for research in the 1990s. In this book, the importance of anthropological approaches to the study of ethnicity will be emphasised. Through its dependence on long-term fieldwork, anthropology has the advantage of generating first-hand knowledge of social life at the level of everyday interaction. To a great extent, this is the locus where ethnicity is created and re-created. Ethnicity emerges and is made relevant through social situations and encounters, and through people's ways of coping with the demands and challenges of life. From its vantage point right at the centre of local life, social anthropology is in a unique position to investigate these processes.

Anthropological approaches also enable us to explore the ways in which ethnic relations are being defined and perceived by people; how

1

they talk and think about their own group as well as other groups, and how particular world views are being maintained or contested. The significance of ethnic membership to people can best be investigated through that detailed on-the-ground research which is the hallmark of anthropology. Finally, social anthropology, as it is a comparative discipline, studies both differences and similarities between ethnic phenomena. It thereby provides a nuanced and complex vision of ethnicity in the contemporary world.

An important reason for the current academic interest in ethnicity and nationalism is the fact that such phenomena have become so visible in many societies that it has become impossible to ignore them. In the early twentieth century, many social theorists held that ethnicity and nationalism would decrease in importance and eventually vanish as a result of modernisation, industrialisation and individualism. This never came about. On the contrary, ethnicity and nationalism have grown in political importance in the world, particularly since the Second World War.

Thirty-five of the thirty-seven major armed conflicts in the world in 1991 were internal conflicts, and most of them – from Sri Lanka to Northern Ireland – could plausibly be described as ethnic conflicts. In addition to violent ethnic movements there are also many important non-violent ethnic movements, such as the Québecois independence movement in Canada. Moreover, in many parts of the world, nation-building – the creation of political cohesion and national identity in former colonies – is high on the political agenda. Ethnic and national identities have also become highly pertinent following the continuous influx of labour migrants and refugees to Europe and North America, which has led to the establishment of new, permanent ethnic minorities in these areas. Since the Second World War, and especially since the 1970s, indigenous populations such as Inuits ('Eskimos') and Sami ('Lapps') have organised themselves politically, and are demanding that their ethnic identities and territorial entitlements should be recognised by the state. Finally, the political turbulence in Europe has moved issues of ethnic and national identities to the forefront of political life. At one extreme of the continent, the erstwhile Soviet Union has split into over a dozen ethnically based states. With the disappearance of the strong socialist state in the countries of Central and Eastern Europe, issues of nationhood and minority problems are emerging with unprecedented force. At the other extreme the reverse seems to be happening, as the nation-states of Western Europe are moving towards a closer economic, political and possibly cultural integration. But here, too, national and ethnic identities have become important issues in recent years. Many people fear the loss of their national or ethnic identity will result from a cultural standardisation following tight European integration. Others, who take a more positive view of such processes, welcome the possibilities for a pan-European identity to replace the ethnic and national ones in a number of contexts, for instance by organising European sports teams and a European army. During the electoral campaign preceding the Danish referendum on European Union in June 1992, a chief anti-EU slogan was: 'I want a country to be European in.' This slogan suggests that personal identities are intimately linked with political processes and that social identities, for example as Danes or Europeans, are not given once and for all, but are negotiated. Both of these insights are crucial to the study of ethnicity.

This book will show how social anthropology can shed light on concrete issues of ethnicity; which questions social anthropologists ask in relation to ethnic phenomena, and how they proceed to answer them. In this way, the book will offer a set of conceptual tools which go far beyond the immediate interpretation of day-to-day politics in their applicability. Some of the questions which will be discussed are:

- How do ethnic groups remain distinctive under different social conditions?
- Under which circumstances does ethnicity become important?
- What is the relationship between ethnic identity and ethnic political organisation?
- Is nationalism always a form of ethnicity?
- What is the relationship between ethnicity and other types of identity, social classification and political organisation, such as class and gender?
- What happens to ethnic relations when societies are industrialised?
- In which ways can history be important in the creation of ethnicity?
- What is the relationship between ethnicity and culture?

This introductory chapter will present the main concepts to be used throughout the book. It also explores their ambiguities and in this way introduces some principal theoretical issues.

The term itself

'Ethnicity seems to be a new term', state Nathan Glazer and Daniel Moynihan (1975: 1), who point to the fact that the word's earliest dictionary appearance is in the *Oxford English Dictionary* in 1972. Its first usage is attributed to the American sociologist David Riesman in 1953. The word 'ethnic', however, is much older. It is derived from the Greek *ethnos* (which in turn derived from the word *ethnikos*), which originally meant heathen or pagan (R. Williams, 1976: 119). It was used in this sense in English from the mid-fourteenth century until the mid-nineteenth century, when it gradually began to refer to 'racial' characteristics. In the United States, 'ethnics' came to be used around the Second World War as a polite term referring to Jews, Italians, Irish and other people considered inferior to the dominant group of largely British descent. None of the founding fathers of sociology and social anthropology – with the partial exception of Max Weber – granted ethnicity much attention.

Since the 1960s, ethnic groups and ethnicity have become household words in Anglophone social anthropology, although, as Ronald Cohen (1978) has remarked, few of those who use the terms bother to define them. In the course of this book, I shall examine a number of approaches to ethnicity. Most of them are closely related, although they may serve different analytical purposes. All of the approaches agree that ethnicity has something to do with the *classification of people* and *group relationships*.

In everyday language the word ethnicity still has a ring of 'minority issues' and 'race relations', but in social anthropology it refers to aspects of relationships between groups which consider themselves, and are regarded by others, as being culturally distinctive. Although it is true that 'the discourse concerning ethnicity tends to concern itself with subnational units, or minorities of some kind or another' (Chapman *et al.*, 1989: 17), majorities and dominant peoples are no less 'ethnic' than minorities. This will be particularly evident in chapters 6 and 7, which discuss nationalism and minority–majority relationships.

Ethnicity, race and nation

A few words must be said initially about the relationship between ethnicity and 'race'. The term race has deliberately been placed within inverted commas in order to stress that it has dubious descriptive value. Whereas it was for some time common to divide humanity into four main races, modern genetics tends not to speak of races. There are two principal reasons for this. First, there has always been so much interbreeding between human populations that it would be meaningless to talk of fixed boundaries between races. Second, the distribution of hereditary physical traits does not follow clear boundaries. In other words, there is often greater variation within a 'racial' group than there is systematic variation between two groups.

Concepts of race can nevertheless be important to the extent that they inform people's actions; at this level, race exists as a cultural construct, whether it has a 'biological' reality or not. Racism, obviously, builds on the assumption that personality is somehow linked with hereditary characteristics which differ systematically between 'races', and in this way race may assume sociological importance even if it has no 'objective' existence. Social scientists who study race relations in Great Britain and the United States need not themselves believe in the existence of race, since their object of study is the social and cultural relevance of the *notion* that race exists. If influential people in a society had developed a similar theory about the hereditary personality traits of red-haired people, and if that theory gained social and cultural significance, 'redhead studies' would for similar reasons have become a field of academic research, even if the researchers themselves did not agree that redheads were different from others in a relevant way. In societies where ideas of race are important, they may therefore be studied as part of local discourses on ethnicity.

Should the study of race relations, in this meaning of the word, be distinguished from the study of ethnicity or ethnic relations? Pierre van den Berghe (1983) does not think so, but would rather regard 'race' relations as a special case of ethnicity. Others, among them Michael Banton (1967), have argued the need to distinguish between race and ethnicity. In Banton's view, race refers to the categorisation of people, while ethnicity has to do with group identification. He argues that ethnicity is generally more concerned with the identification of 'us', while racism is more oriented to the categorisation of 'them' (Banton, 1983, 106: cf. Jenkins, 1986: 177). However, ethnicity can assume many forms, and since ethnic ideologies tend to stress common descent among their members, the distinction between race and ethnicity is a problematic one, even if Banton's distinction between groups and categories can be useful (cf. chapter 3). I shall not, therefore, distinguish between race relations and ethnicity. Ideas of 'race' may or may not form part of ethnic ideologies, and their presence or absence does not seem to be a decisive factor in interethnic relations.

Discrimination on ethnic grounds is spoken of as 'racism' in Trinidad and as 'communalism' in Mauritius (Eriksen, 1992a), but the forms of imputed discrimination referred to can be nearly identical. On the other hand, it is doubtless true that groups who 'look different' from majorities or dominating groups may be less liable to become assimilated into the majority than others, and that it can be difficult for them to escape from their ethnic identity if they wish to. However, this may also hold good for minority groups with, say, an inadequate command of the dominant language. In both cases, their ethnic identity becomes an imperative status, an ascribed aspect of their personhood from which they cannot escape entirely. Race or skin colour as such is not the decisive variable in every society.

The relationship between the terms ethnicity and nationality is nearly as complex as that between ethnicity and race. Like the words ethnic and race, the word nation has a long history (R. Williams, 1976: 213–14) and has been used with a variety of different meanings in English. We shall refrain from discussing these meanings here, and will concentrate on the sense in which nation and nationalism are used analytically in academic discourse. Like ethnic ideologies, nationalism stresses the cultural similarity of its adherents and, by implication, it draws boundaries vis-à-vis others, who thereby become outsiders. The distinguishing mark of nationalism is by definition its relationship to the state. A nationalist holds that political boundaries should be coterminous with cultural boundaries, whereas many ethnic groups do not demand command over a state. When the political leaders of an ethnic movement make demands to this effect, the ethnic movement therefore by definition becomes a nationalist movement. Although nationalisms tend to be ethnic in character, this is not necessarily the case, and we shall look more carefully into the relationship between ethnicity and nationalism in chapters 6 and 7.

Ethnicity and class

The term ethnicity refers to relationships between groups whose members consider themselves distinctive, and these groups may be ranked hierarchically within a society. It is therefore necessary to distinguish clearly between ethnicity and social class.

In the literature of social science, there are two main definitions of classes. One derives from Karl Marx, the other from Max Weber. Sometimes elements from the two definitions are combined.

The Marxist view of social classes emphasises economic aspects. A social class is defined according to its relationship to the productive process in society. In capitalist societies, according to Marx, there are three main classes. First, there is the capitalist class or bourgeoisie, whose members own the means of production (factories, tools and machinery and so on) and buy other people's labour-power (employ them). Second, there is the petit-bourgeoisie, whose members own means of production but do not employ others. Owners of small shops are typical examples. The third and most numerous class is the proletariat or working class, whose members depend upon selling their labour-power to a capitalist for their livelihood. There are also other classes, notably the aristocracy, whose members live by land interest, and the lumpenproletariat, which consists of unemployed and underemployed people – vagrants and the like.

Since Marx's time in the mid-nineteenth century, the theory of classes has been developed in several directions. Its adherents nevertheless still stress the relationship to property in their delineation of classes. A further central feature of this theory is the notion of class struggle. Marx and his followers held that oppressed classes would eventually rise against their oppressors, overthrow them through a revolution, and alter the political order and the social organisation of labour. This, in Marx's view, was the chief way in which societies evolved.

The Weberian view of social classes, which has partly developed into theories of social stratification, combines several criteria in delineating classes, including income, education and political influence. Unlike Marx, Weber did not regard classes as potential corporate groups; he did not believe that members of social classes necessarily would have shared political interests. Weber preferred to speak of 'status groups' rather than classes.

Theories of social class always refer to systems of social ranking and distribution of power. Ethnicity, on the contrary, does not necessarily refer to rank; ethnic relations may well be egalitarian in this regard. Still, many polyethnic societies are ranked according to ethnic membership. The criteria for such ranking are nevertheless different from class ranking: they refer to imputed cultural differences or 'races', not to property or achieved statuses.

There may be a high *correlation* between ethnicity and class, which means that there is a high likelihood that persons belonging to specific ethnic groups also belong to specific social classes. There can be a significant interrelationship between class and ethnicity, both class and ethnicity can be criteria for rank, and ethnic membership can be an important factor in class membership. Both class differences and ethnic differences can be pervasive features of societies, but they are not one and the same thing and must be distinguished from one another analytically.

The current concern with ethnicity

If one runs a word-search programme through a representative sample of English-language anthropological publications since 1950, one will note significant changes in the frequency of a number of key words. Words like 'structure' and 'function', for example, have gradually grown unfashionable, whereas Marxist terms like 'base and superstructure', 'means of production' and 'class struggle' were popular from around 1965 until the early 1980s. Terms like 'ethnicity', 'ethnic' and 'ethnic group', for their part, have steadily grown in currency since the mid- to late 1960s. There may be two main causes for this. One of them is change in the social world, while the other concerns changes in the dominant way of thinking in social anthropology.

Whereas classic social anthropology, as exemplified in the works of Malinowski, Boas, Radcliffe-Brown, Lévi-Strauss, Evans-Pritchard and others, would characteristically focus on single 'tribal' societies, changes in the world after the Second World War have brought many of these societies into increased contact with each other, with the state and with global society. Many of the peoples studied by social anthropologists have become involved in national liberation movements or ethnic conflicts in post-colonial states. Many of them, formerly regarded as 'tribes' or 'aboriginals', have become 'ethnic minorities'. Furthermore, many former members of tribal or traditional groups have migrated to Europe or North America, where their relationships with the host societies have been studied extensively by sociologists, social psychologists and social anthropologists.

Some ethnic groups have moved to towns or regional centres where they are brought into contact with people with other customs, languages and identities, and where they frequently enter into competitive relationships in politics and the labour market. Frequently, people who migrate try to maintain their old kinship and neighbourhood social networks in the new urban context, and both ethnic quarters and ethnic political groupings often emerge in such urban settings. Although the speed of social and cultural change can be high, people tend to retain their ethnic identity despite having moved to a new environment. This kind of social change has been investigated in a series of pioneering studies in North American cities from the 1920s and in Southern Africa from the early 1940s, and we will return to these studies in the next chapter.

In an influential study of ethnic identity in the United States, Glazer and Moynihan (1963) stated that the most important point to be made about the 'American melting-pot' is that it never occurred. They argued that rather than eradicating ethnic differences, modern American society has actually created a new form of self-awareness in people, which is expressed in a concern about roots and origins. Moreover, many Americans continue to use their ethnic networks actively when looking for jobs or a spouse. Many prefer to live in neighbourhoods dominated by people with the same origins as themselves, and they continue to regard themselves as 'Italians', 'Poles' and so on in addition to being Americans – two generations or more after their ancestors left the country of origin.

An important insight from anthropological research has been that ethnic organisation and identity, rather than being 'primordial' phenomena radically opposed to modernity and the modern state, are frequently reactions to processes of modernisation. As Jonathan Friedman has put it, '[e]thnic and cultural fragmentation and modernist homogenization are not two arguments, two opposing views of what is happening in the world today, but two constitutive trends of global reality' (Friedman, 1990: 311).

Does this mean that ethnicity is chiefly a *modern* phenomenon? This is a tricky but highly relevant question. The contemporary ethnic processes referred to above can be described as modern in character. In an influential statement on political ethnicity, Abner Cohen (1974a) has argued that the concept is perhaps most useful in the study of the development of new political cultures in situations of social change in the so-called Third World. However, important studies of ethnicity have been carried out in non-modern, non-Western societies as well.

The contemporary concern with ethnicity and ethnic processes is partly related to historical changes such as the ones mentioned above. It could nevertheless also be argued that the growing interest in ethnicity reflects changes in the dominant anthropological mode of thought. Instead of viewing 'societies' or even 'cultures' as more or less isolated, static and homogeneous units as the early structural-functionalists would have tended to do, many anthropologists now try to depict flux and process, ambiguity and complexity in their analyses of social worlds. In this context, ethnicity has proven a highly useful concept, since it suggests a dynamic situation of variable contact and mutual accommodation between groups.

From tribe to ethnic group

As already mentioned, there has been a shift in Anglophone social anthropological terminology concerning the nature of the social units we study. While one formerly spoke of 'tribes', the term 'ethnic group' is nowadays much more common. Ronald Cohen remarks: 'Quite suddenly, with little comment or ceremony, ethnicity is an ubiquitous presence' (R. Cohen, 1978: 379). This switch in terminology implies more than a mere replacement of one word with another. Notably, the use of the term 'ethnic group' suggests contact and interrelationship. To speak of an ethnic group in total isolation is as absurd as to speak of the sound from one hand clapping (cf. Bateson, 1979: 78). By definition, ethnic groups remain more or less discrete, but they are aware of – and in contact with – members of other ethnic groups. Moreover, these groups or categories are in a sense *created* through that very contact. Group identities must always be defined in relation to that which they are not – in other words, in relation to non-members of the group.

The terminological switch from 'tribe' to 'ethnic group' may also mitigate or even transcend an ethnocentric or Eurocentric bias which anthropologists have often been accused of promoting covertly. When we talk of tribes, we implicitly introduce a sharp, qualitative distinction between ourselves and the people we study; the distinction generally corresponds to the distinction between modern and traditional or so-called primitive societies. If we instead talk of ethnic groups or categories, such a sharp distinction becomes difficult to maintain. Virtually every human being belongs to an ethnic group, whether he or she lives in Europe, Melanesia or Central America. There are ethnic groups in English cities, in the Bolivian countryside and in the New Guinea highlands. Anthropologists themselves belong to ethnic groups or nations. Moreover, the concepts and models used in the study of ethnicity can often be applied to modern as well as non-modern contexts, to Western as well as non-Western societies. In this sense, the concept of ethnicity can be said to bridge two important gaps in social anthropology: it entails a focus on dynamics rather than statics, and it relativises the boundaries between 'Us' and 'Them', between moderns and tribals.

What is ethnicity?

When we talk of ethnicity, we indicate that groups and identities have developed in mutual contact rather than in isolation. But what is the nature of such groups?

When A.L. Kroeber and Clyde Kluckhohn investigated the various meanings of 'culture' in the early 1950s (Kroeber and Kluckhohn, 1952), they found about 300 different definitions. Although Ronald Cohen is correct in stating that most of whose who write on ethnicity do not bother to define the term, the extant number of definitions is already high – and it is growing (B. Williams, 1989). Instead of going through the various definitions of ethnicity here, I will point out significant differences between theoretical perspectives as we go along. As a starting point, let us examine the recent development of the term as it is used by social anthropologists.

The term 'ethnic group' has come to mean something like 'a people'. But what is 'a people'? Does the population of Britain constitute a people, does it comprise several peoples (as Nairn, 1977, tends to argue), or does it rather form part of a Germanic, or an English-speaking, or a European people? All of these positions may have their defenders, and this very ambiguity in the designation of peoples has been taken on as a challenge by anthropologists. In a study of ethnic relations in Thailand, Michael Moerman (1965) asks himself: 'Who are the Lue?' The Lue were the ethnic group his research focused on, but when he tried to describe who they were – in which ways they were distinctive from other ethnic groups – he quickly ran into trouble. His problem, a very common one in contemporary social anthropology, concerned the boundaries of the group. After listing a number of criteria commonly used by anthropologists to demarcate cultural groups, such as language, political organisation and territorial contiguity, he states: 'Since language, culture, political organization, etc., do not correlate completely, the units delimited by one criterion do not coincide with the units delimited by another' (Moerman, 1965: 1215). When he asked individual Lue what were their typical characteristics, they would mention cultural traits which they in fact shared with other, neighbouring groups. They lived in close interaction with other groups in the area; they had no exclusive livelihood, no exclusive language, no exclusive customs, no exclusive religion. Why was it appropriate to describe them as an ethnic group? After posing these problems, Moerman was forced to conclude that '[s]omeone is Lue by virtue of believing and calling himself Lue and of acting in ways that validate his Lueness' (Moerman, 1965: 1219). Being unable to argue that this 'Lueness' can be defined with reference to objective cultural features or clear-cut boundaries, Moerman defines it as an *emic category of ascription*.[1] This way of delineating ethnic groups has become very influential in social anthropology (cf. chapter 3).

Does this imply that ethnic groups do not necessarily have a distinctive culture? Can two groups be culturally identical and yet constitute two different ethnic groups? This is a complicated question, which will be dealt with at length in later chapters. At this point we should note that, contrary to a widespread commonsense view, cultural difference between two groups is not the decisive feature of ethnicity. Two distinctive, endogamous groups, say, somewhere in New Guinea, may well have widely different languages, religious beliefs and even technologies, but that does not necessarily mean that there is an ethnic relationship between them. For ethnicity to come about, the groups must have a minimum of contact with each other, and they must entertain ideas of each other as being culturally

---

1 In the anthropological literature, the term *emic* refers to 'the native's point of view'. It is contrasted with *etic*, which refers to the analyst's concepts, descriptions and analyses. The terms are derived from phonemics and phonetics.

different from themselves. If these conditions are not fulfilled, there is no ethnicity, for ethnicity is essentially an aspect of a relationship, not a property of a group[2]. This is a key point. Conversely, some groups may seem culturally similar, yet there can be a socially highly relevant (and even volatile) interethnic relationship between them. This would be the case of the relationship between Serbs and Croats following the break-up of Yugoslavia, or of the tension between coastal Sami and Norwegians. There may also be considerable cultural variation within a group without ethnicity (Blom, 1969). Only in so far as cultural differences are perceived as being important, and are made socially relevant, do social relationships have an ethnic element.

Ethnicity is an aspect of social relationship between agents who consider themselves as culturally distinctive from members of other groups with whom they have a minimum of regular interaction. It can thus also be defined as a social identity (based on a contrast vis-à-vis others) characterised by metaphoric or fictive kinship (Yelvington, 1991: 168). When cultural differences regularly make a difference in interaction between members of groups, the social relationship has an ethnic element. Ethnicity refers both to aspects of gain and loss in interaction, and to aspects of meaning in the creation of identity. In this way it has a political, organisational aspect as well as a symbolic one.

Ethnic groups tend to have myths of common origin and they nearly always have ideologies encouraging endogamy, which may nevertheless be of highly varying practical importance.

'Kinds' of ethnic relations?

This very general and tentative definition of ethnicity lumps together a great number of very different social phenomena. My relationship with my Pakistani greengrocer has an ethnic aspect; so, it could be argued, do the war in former Yugoslavia and 'race riots' in American cities. Do these phenomena have anything interesting in common, justifying their comparison within a single conceptual framework? The answer is both yes and no.

One of the contentions from anthropological studies of ethnicity is that there may be mechanisms of ethnic processes which are relatively uniform in every interethnic situation: to this effect, we can identify certain shared formal properties in all ethnic phenomena.

---

2 Glazer & Moynihan (1975: 1) nevertheless define ethnicity as 'the character or quality of an ethnic group'. The advantages of regarding it as an aspect of a relationship instead will be shown in later chapters.

On the other hand, there can be no doubt that the substantial social contexts of ethnicity differ enormously, and indeed that ethnic identities and ethnic organisations themselves may have highly variable importance in different societies, for different individuals and in different situations. We should nevertheless keep in mind that the point of anthropological comparison is not necessarily to establish similarities between societies; it can also reveal important differences. In order to discover such differences, we must initially possess some kind of measuring stick, a constant or a conceptual bridgehead, which can be used as a basis of comparison. If we first know what we mean by ethnicity, we can then use the concept as a common denominator for societies and social contexts which are otherwise very different. The concept of ethnicity can in this way not only teach us something about similarity, but also about differences.

Although the concept of ethnicity should always have the same meaning lest it ceases to be useful in comparison, it is inevitable that we distinguish between the social contexts under scrutiny. Some interethnic contexts in different societies are very similar and may seem easily comparable, whereas others differ profoundly. In order to give an idea of the variation, I shall briefly describe some typical empirical foci of ethnic studies, some kinds of ethnic groups, so to speak. This list is not exhaustive.

(a) Urban ethnic minorities. This category would include, among others, non-European immigrants in European cities and Hispanics in the United States, as well as migrants to industrial towns in Africa and elsewhere. Research on immigrants has focused on problems of adaptation, on ethnic discrimination from the host society, racism, and issues relating to identity management and cultural change (cf. chapters 4 and 7). Anthropologists who have investigated urbanisation in Africa have focused on change and continuity in political organisation and social identity following migration to totally new settings (cf. chapter 2). Although they have political interests, these ethnic groups rarely demand political independence or statehood, and they are as a rule integrated into a capitalist system of production and consumption.

(b) Indigenous peoples. This word is a blanket term for aboriginal inhabitants of a territory, who are politically relatively powerless and who are only partly integrated into the dominant nation-state. Indigenous peoples are associated with a non-industrial mode of production and a stateless political system (Minority Rights Group, 1990). The Basques of the Bay of Biscay and the Welsh of Great Britain are not considered indigenous populations, although they are certainly as indigenous, technically speaking, as the Sami of northern Scandinavia or the Jívaro of the Amazon basin. The concept 'indigenous people' is thus not an accurate analytical one, but rather one drawing on broad family resemblances and contemporary political issues (cf. chapters 4 and 7).

(c) Proto-nations (so-called ethnonationalist movements). These groups, the most famous of ethnic groups in the news media of the 1990s, include Kurds, Sikhs, Palestinians and Sri Lankan Tamils, and their number is growing. By definition, these groups have political leaders who claim that they are entitled to their own nation-state and should not be 'ruled by others'. These groups, short of having a nation-state, may be said to have more substantial characteristics in common with nations (cf. chapter 6) than with either urban minorities or indigenous peoples. They are always territorially based; they are differentiated according to class and educational achievement, and they are large groups. In accordance with common terminology, these groups may be described as 'nations without a state'. Anthropologists have studied such movements in a number of societies, including Euzkadi or the Basque country (Heiberg, 1989), Brittany (McDonald, 1989) and Québec (Handler, 1988).

(d Ethnic groups in 'plural societies'. The term 'plural society' usually designates colonially created states with culturally heterogeneous populations (Furnivall, 1948; M.G. Smith, 1965). Typical plural societies would be Kenya, Indonesia and Jamaica. The groups that make up the plural society, although they are compelled to participate in uniform political and economic systems, are regarded as (and regard themselves as) highly distinctive in other matters. In plural societies, secessionism is usually not an option and ethnicity tends to be articulated as group competition. As Richard Jenkins (1986) has remarked, most contemporary states could plausibly be considered plural ones.

The definition of ethnicity proposed earlier would include all of these 'kinds' of groups, no matter how different they are in other respects. Surely, there are aspects of politics (gain and loss in interaction) as well as meaning (social identity and belonging) in the ethnic relations reproduced by urban minorities, indigenous peoples, proto-nations and the component groups of plural societies alike. Despite the great variations between the problems and substantial characteristics represented by the respective kinds of groups, the term ethnicity may, in other words, meaningfully be used as a common denominator for them. In later chapters, it will be shown how anthropological approaches to ethnicity may shed light on both similarities and differences between different social contexts and historical circumstances.

Analytical concepts and 'native' concepts

The final problem to be discussed in this chapter concerns the relationship between anthropological concepts and their subject-matter. This is a problem with complicated ramifications, and it concerns the relationships between (i) anthropological theory and 'native theory', (ii) anthropological theory and social organisation, and (iii) 'native theory' and social organisation.

It can be argued that the terminological shift from 'tribe' to 'ethnic group' mitigated the formerly strong distinction between 'moderns' and 'primitives'. The growing anthropological interest in nationalism entails a further step towards 'studying ourselves'. For if ethnicity can be non-modern as well as modern, nationalism must be identified with the modern age, with the French Enlightenment and German Romanticism as parallel starting points. Nationalist slogans, movements and symbols have later penetrated into the heartlands of anthropological research. Nationalism, as it is a modern state ideology, is present in the social worlds in which the anthropologists themselves live. Although there are interesting differences between particular nationalisms, nationalism as such is a modern ideology. When studying nationalism in a foreign country, it is therefore difficult to use one's own society as an implicit contrast as anthropologists have frequently done when studying what they regard as exotic societies. In fact, as Richard Handler (1988) has observed, nationalism and social science, including anthropology, grew out of the same historical circumstances of modernisation, industrialisation and the growth of individualism in the nineteenth century. For this reason, Handler argues, it has been difficult for anthropologists to attain sufficient analytical distance vis-à-vis nationalisms; the respective concepts and ways of thinking are too closely related (cf. also Herzfeld, 1987; Just, 1989).

Handler's point is also valid in relation to modern ethnopolitical movements. Those who speak for these movements tend to invoke a concept of culture which is in fact often directly inspired by anthropological concepts of culture, and in some cases they self-consciously present themselves as 'tribes' reminiscent of the 'tribes' depicted in classical anthropological monographs (Roosens, 1989). In these cases, there is an intrinsic relationship between anthropological theorising and 'native theory'. Additionally, when anthropologists study contested issues in their own societies, there is a real risk that the scholarly conceptual apparatus will be contaminated by the inaccurate and perhaps ideologically loaded everyday meanings of the words. For this reason, we should be particularly cautious in our choice of analytical terms and interpretations when we study phenomena such as ethnicity and nationalism.

The points made by Handler and others in relation to the study of nationalism and modern ethnopolitics can nevertheless be seen as general problems of social anthropology. The main problem concerns how to articulate the relationship between anthropological theory, 'native theory' and social organisation (Mitchell, 1974). In a sense, ethnicity is created by the analyst when he or she goes out into the world and poses questions about ethnicity. Had one instead been concerned with gender, one would doubtless have found aspects of gender instead of ethnicity. On the other hand, individuals or informants who live in the societies in question may themselves be concerned with issues relating to ethnicity, and as such the phenomenon clearly does exist outside of the mind of the observer. But since our concepts, for example ethnicity and nationalism, are our own inventions, we must not assume that the actors themselves have the same ideas about the ways in which the world is constituted – even if they are using the very same words as ourselves! History and social identity are constructed socially, sometimes with a very tenuous relationship with established, or at least official, facts (cf. chapter 4).

There are often discrepancies between what people say and what they do, and there will nearly always be discrepancies between informants' descriptions of their society and the anthropologist's description of the same society. Indeed, many anthropologists (for instance Holy and Stuchlik, 1983) hold that it is a chief goal of our discipline to investigate and clarify the relationship between notions and actions, or between what people say and what they do. One may disagree with their 'rationalist' perspective, which seems to assume that a simple, 'economic' means–end rationality underlies all social action, but the general problem remains important: why is it that people say one thing and then proceed to do something entirely different, and how can this be investigated?

This discrepancy is relevant for ethnic studies, and it requires that we are clear about the distinctions between our own concepts and models, 'native' concepts and models, and social process. In some societies, people will perhaps deny that there is systematic differential treatment between members of different groups, although the anthropologist will discover that such discrimination exists.

Conversely, I have met many Christians during fieldwork who have sworn, in conversations, that they would (for ostensibly sound reasons) have nothing to do with Muslims; later on, it has turned out that they in fact entertain quite strong and sometimes confidential relationships with Muslims. It is, indeed, frequently contradictions of this kind that lead to anthropological insights.

2 ETHNIC CLASSIFICATION: US AND THEM

He came of good class, had a light olive complexion and hair with large waves ('good' hair, Miss Henery thought of it as; as a member of the West Indian coloured middle class, she conceived of human hair in terms of 'good' and 'bad' – sometimes 'good' and 'hard'; 'good' hair is hair that is European in appearance; 'bad' or 'hard' hair is of the kinky, negroid type).

Edgar Mittelholzer (1979: 58)

The first fact of ethnicity is the application of systematic distinctions between insiders and outsiders; between Us and Them. If no such principle exists there can be no ethnicity, since ethnicity presupposes an institutionalised relationship between delineated categories whose members consider each other to be culturally distinctive. From this principle, it follows that two or several groups who regard themselves as being distinctive may tend to become more similar *and* simultaneously increasingly concerned with their distinctiveness if their mutual contact increases. Ethnicity is thus constituted through social contact. This chapter will present general aspects of these processes of contact. In later chapters, wider contexts for ethnic relations at the interpersonal level will be elucidated – from the formation of ethnic groups (chapter 3) and the creation of ethnic identities and ideologies (chapter 4), to the historical conditions for ethnicity (chapter 5) and the relationship between ethnicity and the state (chapters 6 and 7). Although ethnicity is not wholly created by individual agents, it can simultaneously provide agents with meaning *and* with organisational channels for pursuing their culturally defined interests. It is very important to be aware of this duality.

The ecology of the city

Some of the earliest empirical research on complex polyethnic societies was undertaken by the group which has come to be known as the Chicago School, comprising urban sociologists as well as anthropologists (Park, 1950; cf. Hannerz, 1980). Among the main problems investigated by Robert Park and his associates in the 1920s and 1930s was how it could be that ethnic groups remained distinctive in American cities – and to what extent they did so through time. In other words, they were concerned with continuity and change in ethnic relations. We owe the widespread use of concepts of 'acculturation' and 'the American melting-pot' to the efforts of Park and his colleagues. By acculturation, they meant the adaptation of immigrants to their new cultural context. It could, but did not have to, eventually lead to total assimilation or loss of ethnic distinctiveness.

Park regarded the city as a kind of ecological system with its own internal dynamic, creating diverse opportunities and constraints for different individuals and groups. At the same time it contained several distinct 'social worlds' based on class and 'race' or ethnicity. These social worlds corresponded to distinctive physical neighbourhoods divided by unequal access to economic resources as well as ethnic differences. The combination of economic adaptation and ethnic identity thus created 'natural areas' such as Little Sicily and the 'Black Belt' in Chicago, more or less sharply distinguished from each other through their respective places in the division of labour and the cultural identities of their inhabitants. Economic, political and cultural resources were to a great extent pooled within each ethnic subsystem so that the individual could achieve many of his or her goals through ethnic networks. Mobility within the system as a whole could be achieved through acculturation – the adoption of the white, English-speaking majority's values and ways of life – which in turn depended on the economic success of individuals or groups. 'The typical "race relations" cycle,' remarks Ulf Hannerz (1980: 44) in an assessment of the Chicago School, 'would lead from isolation through competition, conflict, and accommodation to assimilation.'

A main point in Park's work is that every society is a more or less successful melting-pot where diverse populations are merged, acculturated and eventually assimilated, at different rates and in different ways, depending on their place in the economic and political systems.

The melting-pot metaphor

The interethnic contexts investigated by the Chicago School were transient, recently constituted and perhaps atypical. In 1900, almost 80 per cent of Chicago's population consisted of immigrants and their children; as late as 1930, about 35 per cent of the population were foreign-born. Following the 'ethnic revival' of the 1960s and 1970s, it has become commonplace to criticise the notion of the melting-pot for having been empirically wrong since it predicted the demise of ethnicity. As a matter of fact, the critics would maintain, the diverse ethnic groups never merged, and indeed the differences between them seem to have been accentuated after two generations or more of mutual adaptation.

This kind of development (cf. chapter 7) would not have been incomprehensible to Park. He stressed that ethnicity, and ethnic conflict (or race prejudice), was an aspect of the relationship between groups and that it was caused by threats, real or imaginary, to an existing 'ecological pattern' of mutual adjustment. In other words, the social mobility – downwards or upwards – of any ethnic group would lead to tension in relation to the other groups.

Park was also aware of the *fluid* character of ethnic categorisations. As an individual moves between social contexts in the flux and transience of urban life, the relative importance of his or her ethnic membership changes. Thus an 'individual may have many "selves" according to the groups to which he belongs and the extent to which each of these groups is isolated from the others' (Park, 1955 [1921], quoted in Lal, 1986: 290).

These and related insights of the Chicago School have proved to be of lasting value in the study of ethnicity: they showed that ethnic relations are fluid and negotiable; that their importance varies situationally; and that, for all their claims to primordiality and cultural roots, ethnic identities can be consciously manipulated and invested in economic competition in modern societies. As we shall now see, conclusions which were by and large compatible with those of the Chicago School also emerged, slightly later, from anthropological studies of 'tribalism' and interethnic relations in urbanising Southern Africa.

Communicating cultural difference

The intergroup contacts that constitute ethnicity may be caused by a variety of factors, among them population growth, the establishment of new communication technologies facilitating trade, inclusion of new groups in a capitalist system of production and exchange, political change incorporating new groups in a single political system, and/or migration. The following studies exemplify several of these processes.

In the 1930s there was a growing demand for labour in the copper mines in the part of Northern Rhodesia (now Zambia) known as the Copperbelt. This spurred a stream of migration from rural areas to the mining towns, and the workers settled in large barracks. There were several important changes in the social situation of these workers.

They had formerly been subsistence farmers in rural villages; now they had become wage labourers in towns with a predominantly monetary economy. In most cases, their social organisation had formerly been based on kinship; now they were individually tied to the mining enterprise. Most of the workers lived alone in the barracks. If they were married, their families were left behind in the village, at least at the early stages. Finally, they were taking part in a social system of a much larger scale and greater complexity than formerly. Whereas the villagers were more or less self-sufficient and had only sporadic contacts with members of other ethnic groups, as town-dwellers they were in continuous interaction with a large number of individuals from ethnic groups other than their own. They shared housing, working places and leisure facilities with others. In some of the towns, dozens of 'tribes' were represented.

This process of urbanisation was investigated by anthropologists based at the Rhodes-Livingstone Institute in Lusaka. Among the most prominent of these were Godfrey Wilson, Max Gluckman, J. Clyde Mitchell and A.L. Epstein. This group is today known as the Manchester School because of its members' later affiliation with the University of Manchester. Some of their studies, including Wilson's *Essay on the Economics of Detribalization* (G. Wilson, 1941–2), focused almost exclusively on change, whereas others, such as Mitchell's small monograph *The Kalela Dance* (Mitchell, 1956), looked into the relationship between social and cultural change and continuity. Whereas Wilson described what he saw as a process of *detribalisation*, Mitchell argued that a form of *retribalisation* (what we would today call ethnicity) was taking place in the mining towns.

Although kin groups and 'tribes' were economically relatively unimportant in the towns, group membership was emphasised to the extent of being *overcommunicated* (Goffman, 1959) in public rituals as well as in casual interaction. This means that ethnicity was deliberately 'shown off'. In other polyethnic situations ethnicity may rather be *undercommunicated*, which means that the actors try to play it down and not to make it an important aspect of a situation.

Although people in the towns were not socially organised along tribal or ethnic lines, they grew strongly self-conscious of their ethnic identity under these circumstances of extensive contact with others. They developed standardised ways of behaving vis-à-vis each other, and oriented themselves socially according to ethnic 'maps' which would have been quite superfluous in a village setting, where most of one's contacts were intraethnic. Many of the new social subsystems that developed in the urban environment, such as clubs and peer groups assembling in beer-halls, were based on ethnic membership.

Mitchell (1956) focuses on one such new institution, the kalela dance. It was performed every Sunday afternoon in Luanshya by male members of the Bisa category. They were dressed in a modern way, and the dance did not form part of the group's traditional cultural repertoire. However, the kalela dance and accompanying songs were conspicuous and overt markers of group identity: most of the songs ridiculed the other groups and praised the homeland of the Bisa. Similar performances were carried out by other groups as well. In this way people's social identities were established and emphasised in a striking way. In a village setting such rituals would have been unnecessary, both because the inhabitants knew each other and because villages were as a rule mono-ethnic.

Stereotyping

In the Copperbelt, cultural differences were communicated in private situations as well. When two individuals met for the first time, the first information they would gather about one another would be their ethnic membership. When this fact was established they would know roughly how to behave towards each other, since there were standardised relationships between groups. Some groups had a 'friendly' relationship, some had a 'hostile' one, and yet others had 'joking' relationships. If one knew someone's ethnic identity, one would know what kind of behaviour towards them would be appropriate. The members of each group had particular notions about the vices and virtues of the others, and these notions were articulated and dramatised in public rituals such as the kalela dance.

When such notions become part and parcel of the 'cultural knowledge' of a group and thus regularly and more or less predictably guide their relationships with others, we may describe them as ethnic stereotypes. Mitchell explains:

Town-dwellers display their ethnic origin by the language they speak and their way of life generally. This enables members of other tribal groups immediately to fit their neighbours and acquaintances into categories which determine the mode of behaviour towards them. For Africans in the Copperbelt 'tribe' is the primary category of social interaction, i.e. the first significant characteristic to which any African reacts in another. (Mitchell, 1956: 32)

Stereotypes are often mentioned in connection with racism and discrimination, so that, for example, white Americans may justify discrimination against blacks by referring to the latter's 'lazy and erratic ways'. Stereotypes tend to be more or less pejorative, although this is not necessarily the case. Many Europeans have positive stereotypes of 'primitive peoples', arguing that their quality of life is higher than their own. Used analytically in social anthropology, the concept of stereotyping refers to the creation and consistent application of standardised notions of the cultural distinctiveness of a group. Stereotypes are held by dominated groups as well as by dominating ones, and they are widespread in societies with siginficant power differences as well as in societies where there is a rough power equilibrium between ethnic groups. In most polyethnic societies, ethnic stereotypes exist, although there always exist individuals who do not hold such stereotypes – as well as individuals who are acknowledged to be 'exceptions'.

In the polyethnic Indian Ocean island society of Mauritius, the entire population of 1 million consists of the descendants of immigrants who have arrived in successive waves since the French colonisation in 1715. The most important ethnic categories are Hindus and Muslims (of Indian descent), Creoles (of largely African and Malagasy descent), Coloureds (of 'mixed' descent), Sino-Mauritians (of Chinese descent) and Franco-Mauritians (of French and British descent). The groups tend to have mutual stereotypes of each other and of themselves (Eriksen, 1988; 1992a). The most important of these stereotypes are summarised in Figure 2.1.

STEREOTYPES HELD BY OTHERS

Creoles	Lazy, merry, careless
Hindus	Stingy, dishonest, hardworking
Muslims	Religious fanatics, non-minglers
Sino-Mauritians	Greedy, industrious
Franco-Mauritians	Snobbish, decadent, undemocratic
Coloureds	Clever, conceited, too ambitious

STEREOTYPES OF SELF

Creoles	Funloving, compassionate, friendly
Hindus	Sensible, care for family
Muslims	Members of a proud, expanding culture
Sino-Mauritians	Clever, industrious
Franco-Mauritians	'True Mauritian', dignified
Coloureds	'True Mauritian', intelligent

Figure 2.1: Mauritian ethnic stereotypes Source: Eriksen, 1988.

Here, we should keep in mind that actual interethnic relations may very well diverge from stereotypes as they are presented in conversations; that there may be a discrepancy between what people say and what they do. In a famous study of the relationship between attitudes and actions in the US, La Piere (1934) toured the American West Coast with a Chinese couple and visited a large number of restaurants and hotels with them. They were refused service only once. He then sent out a questionnaire to the owners of the establishments, asking them whether or not they would accept 'members of the Chinese race' as guests. The vast majority affirmed that they would not.

Stereotypes need not be true, and they do not necessarily give good descriptions of what people actually do. Therefore, we must reflect on the causes and uses of stereotypes.

First of all, in Mauritius as well as in the Copperbelt, stereotypes help the individual to create order in an otherwise excruciatingly complicated social universe. They make it possible to divide the social world into *kinds* of people, and they provide simple criteria for such a classification. They give the individual the impression that he or she understands society.

Second, stereotypes can justify privileges and differences in access to a society's resources. Conversely, negative stereotypes directed towards a ruling group may alleviate feelings of powerlessness and resignation: they can be seen as the symbolic revenge of the downtrodden.

Third, stereotypes are crucial in defining the boundaries of one's own group. They inform the individual of the virtues of his or her own group and the vices of the others, and they thereby serve to justify thinking that 'I am an X and not a Y.' In the vast majority of cases stereotypes imply, in some way or other, the superiority of one's own group. However, there are also minorities who have largely negative stereotypes of themselves and positive ones of the dominating group.

Stereotypes can sometimes function as self-fulfilling prophecies. A dominating group can stunt the intellectual development of a dominated group by systematically telling them that they are inferior. There are, of course, many stereotypes which have little or no truth, such as the ideas commonly held by many African peoples and others to the effect that their neighbours are cannibals (Arens, 1978).

Finally, stereotypes can be morally ambiguous and contested by different parties. In Mauritius, it is often said that 'If a Creole has ten rupees, he will spend fifteen; but if a Hindu has ten rupees, he spends seven and hoards the rest.' This saying is sometimes invoked by Creoles as well as Hindus as proof of their own community's moral superiority.

The moral character of stereotyping is not the main point here. Rather, it should be stressed that stereotypes contribute to defining one's own group in relation to others by providing a tidy 'map' of the social world, and that they can justify systematic differences in access to resources.

Folk taxonomies, social distance

As noted above, informal groupings in the Copperbelt tended to be based on ethnic membership. For example, a vast majority of town-dwellers chose drinking companions from their own 'tribe' or ethnic category. In the barracks, they preferred to have room mates from their own group. However, if this was not possible they would rather share their room with people whom they perceived as close than with people they perceived as distant (Mitchell, 1974). Perceptions of distance, Mitchell notes, combined cultural and geographic criteria so that, for example, matrilineal peoples from the north would rank other matrilineal peoples from the north as those closest to themselves. In a large survey of townspeople (which was probably male-biased), Mitchell and his assistants used the following scale of 'stages of social distance or social nearness':

1. Would admit him to near kinship by marriage.
2. Would share a meal with him.
3. Would work together with him.
4. Would allow to live nearby in my village.
5. Would allow to settle in my tribal area.
6. Would allow as a visitor only in my tribal area.
7. Would exclude from my tribal area.
(Mitchell, 1956: 23)[1]

On the basis of such perceptions of social distance, the town-dwellers developed – and reconfirmed, through interaction – a system of social classification where one did not just distinguish between Us and Them, but where there were various degrees of group inclusion and exclusion. In other words, there were different Us and Them groups. Depending on the situation, different levels of group membership could be activated. For instance, in local politics an

1 This kind of categorisation is based on the Bogardus social distance scale, used in research on ethnicity in American cities by the Chicago School. The original categories were: (1) Would marry. (2) Would have as a regular friend. (3) Would work beside in an office. (4) Would have several families in my neighbourhood. (5) Would have merely as speaking acquaintances. (6) Would have live outside my neighbourhood. (7) Would have live outside my country.

individual would behave as a member of a larger group than he or she would concerning questions of marriage.

I have explored the functioning of ethnic classification in Mauritius, which officially has four ethnic 'communities'; that is to say, the Constitution of Mauritius acknowledges the existence of four communities: Hindus (52 per cent), Muslims (16 per cent), Sino-Mauritians or Chinese (3 per cent) and 'general population' (29 per cent). The general population is a residual category which encompasses people of African, European and mixed descent. Nearly all of them are Catholics, but they do not consider themselves an ethnic group. They rarely intermarry and do not vote together at elections. Moreover, it transpires that the 'Hindus' cannot be considered an ethnic group either, especially since this category includes both Biharis from north India (the most numerous segment) and a fair proportion of Tamils and Telugus, who do not identify themselves as members of the same ethnic group as the northerners.

It is impossible to tell straightforwardly how many ethnic groups exist in Mauritius. Cultural differences are communicated in a variety of situations, but they do not always refer to the same social distinctions. A Mauritian Hindu, for example, can be morally compelled to marry at the caste level, but will usually vote for the party representing all (northern) Hindus. Further, distinctions are made between groups whose existence is ignored by other Mauritians, such as when Creoles distinguish between Rodriguais (from Mauritius' dependency, Rodrigues) and Mauritian Creoles. Similarly, Mauritian Tamils would distinguish between urban and rural Tamils, sometimes to the extent of discouraging intermarriage, but such a distinction is not widely known outside of the Tamil 'community'. To the question of 'how many ethnic groups exist in Mauritius?', therefore, we must reply that this depends on the situation.

As a general rule, ethnic folk taxonomies are at their most detailed closest to the actor. To a white Franco-Mauritian, it is of little consequence that Shi'ite and Sunni Muslims do not intermarry, or that there is little political loyalty between Marathis and Biharis (both of them Hindus). To the agents themselves, such distinctions may be of great importance in practical matters as well as in matters relating to identity and definition of self in relation to others.

Dichotomisation and complementarisation

Many studies of ethnicity have stressed the relative distinctiveness of ethnic groups. Very often it is taken for granted that the groups in a polyethnic social system remain apart and different in most regards, and a great number of studies focus on the ways in which the groups manage to remain discrete (see chapter 3). However, since ethnicity is an aspect of relationship, one may equally well stress the mutual contact and the integrative aspect. To some extent this was emphasised in Fredrik Barth's early study of ethnic 'niches' in Swat, where the biological metaphor of symbiosis was used to describe group relations (Barth, 1956), and it was a central point in the Chicago School (for example Wirth, 1956 [1928]) that the degree of isolation varied in interethnic relationships. Barth showed how the three ethnic groups of Swat valley (in north Pakistan), the Pathans, the Kohistanis and the Gujars, had adapted economically not only to the natural environment but also to the human aspect of their environment; that is to say, to each other. They had gradually developed mutual interdependencies through trade, exchanging necessities and services each of them had specialised in providing. The transhumant mountain Gujars, for example, depended on the lowland Pathans for fodder, while the Pathans bought dairy products from the Gujars.

In Harald Eidheim's (1971) studies of the Sami in northern Norway, processes of interethnic accommodation are described in great detail at the level of interaction. Eidheim shows how negative stereotyping can be interrelated with a shared cultural repertoire – indeed, that both aspects are probably necessary components of a stable system of interethnic relations.

Group membership and loyalties are confirmed and strengthened through stereotyping and the articulation of conflict or competition between Sami and Norwegians. This mutual demarcation process can be called 'dichotomisation'.

For interethnic interaction to take place at all, however, there must be some mutual recognition inherent in the process of communicating cultural differences. Otherwise, the ethnic identity of at least one of the parties will necessarily be neglected and undercommunicated in a situation of interaction. Such an acknowledgement of differences can be labelled 'complementarisation'. Here, the cultural differences communicated through ethnicity are considered a fact and frequently an asset. Whereas dichotomisation essentially expresses an Us–Them kind of relationship, complementarisation can be described as a We–You kind of process. When one enters an interethnic relationship, it is necessary to establish a field of complementarity. This could be a shared language within which interaction can take place.

In relation to power, complementarisation can lead to two opposite results. Indigenous and other minority movements which seek recognition by the majority may try to establish an ideology of complementarity in order to be able to negotiate on an equal footing with the majority. On the other hand, dominant groups may also speak of complementarity in order to justify exploitation of and discrimination against minorities. This may be particularly relevant in societies with an ethnic division of labour, where, for example, particular ethnic groups carry out most of the underpaid manual work. In such situations, dominant groups may emphasise that it is the 'nature' of the members of group X to do manual work; that they are 'unsuitable' – by nature or by culture – to carry out prestigious jobs. The former apartheid system of South Africa exemplifies this hierarchical kind of complementarity.

An important point demonstrated by the preceding discussion is that interethnic relations are not necessarily conflictual. Although there are frequently discrepancies of power (in Swat, the Pathans are clearly the dominant group), interethnic systems of communication and/or exchange may well be based on cooperation and mutual acknowledgement. Indeed, if there is little complementarisation in interethnic relations, there will usually be a tendency towards identity shift or assimilation among members of the weaker group. To sum up: ethnicity entails the establishment of both Us–Them contrasts (dichotomisation) *and* a shared field for interethnic discourse and interaction (complementarisation).

Ethnic stigma

Although it has scarcely been accorded a central place in the anthropological study of ethnicity, it is a fact that many interethnic relations are highly asymmetrical regarding access to political power and economic resources. It therefore seems appropriate at this point to present an interethnic relationship which has for centuries been marked by clearly hierarchical aspects.

Unlike the transhumant Sami of the mountain tundra of northern Scandinavia, the Sami of the Norwegian Arctic coast are not reindeer herders. Like the Norwegians who live in the same area, they obtain their livelihood from fishing and agriculture. The two populations have been in contact for many centuries. They occupy the same economic niche, they live in the same kinds of houses, wear the same kind of clothing and practise the same Protestant religion. Upon arriving in one of these mixed communities, Eidheim (1969; 1971) looked in vain for cultural traits distinguishing Sami from Norwegians. During the first months of his fieldwork, the locals took great pains to show off their Norwegianness. They always spoke the local Norwegian dialect. The housewives had what to Eidheim seemed a craze for cleanliness. (Uncleanliness is considered a typical Sami vice by Norwegians.) On the face of it, there were no Sami in the community. However, although 'there is a conspicuous lack of "contrasting cultural traits" between ... [Sami] and Norwegians, ... these ethnic labels are attached to communities as well as to families and individual persons, and are in daily use' (Eidheim, 1971: 51).

Gradually some of Eidheim's informants took him into their confidence, realising that he, a southerner and an unusual one at that, had no stake in the local interethnic system. As he grew to know them better, it turned out that many of the locals habitually spoke Sami (a language unrelated to Norwegian) at home. Indeed, a majority of the fjord population were Sami. However, it was impossible to engage people in conversations about ethnicity in public. In such situations, at the shop or at the quay for example, people would always act emphatically Norwegian. They would certainly speak Norwegian in such situations.

In this part of the country the Sami have traditionally been the weaker party in a patron–client relationship, and they were considered primitive, backward, stupid and dirty by the dominant Norwegians. Therefore, Sami ethnic identity was consistently *undercommunicated* in public situations. Conversely, their command of modern Norwegian culture was strongly *overcommunicated*; they presented themselves as Norwegians to others. Sami identity became a kind of secret. Still, everybody in the community knew who was 'really' a Sami and who was not. Thus a total identity change was nearly impossible in the short run (say, within an individual's lifetime), even if there were few 'objective cultural differences' between Sami and Norwegians. Since it was connected with undesirable and presumably immutable personality traits, Sami identity could be described as a stigmatised identity. Being recognised as a Sami entailed that one was considered inferior to Norwegians, and this, of course, was the main reason why Sami identity was being undercommunicated. Moreover, many Sami themselves shared the dominant, pejorative view of Sami culture, and refused to teach their children Sami. This kind of self-contempt is characteristic of powerless groups in polyethnic contexts.

The mountain Sami have gone through a process of ethnic *incorporation*: they have organised themselves politically on an ethnic basis. This coastal Sami population has rather moved towards *assimilation*, gradually losing their markers of distinctiveness and merging into the majority population. Eventually, it seemed at the time of Eidheim's fieldwork, the descendants of these Sami would become Norwegian, just like the inhabitants of many small fishing communities on this coast, which were formerly Sami but which are now –

after generations of cultural 'Norwegianisation' – considered Norwegian. This kind of process is very common among discriminated minorities, but it presupposes that there is a real, practical possibility of removing the stigma imposed by the dominant population. If, for example, the Sami had been physically very different from the Norwegians, the process of assimilation would probably have been more difficult.

It should be noted, however, that many coastal Sami have remained 'split' between Norwegian and Sami identities in a sometimes problematic way. Aware of their Sami ancestry and of the fact that their grandparents (and sometimes parents) had a way of life that was very distinctive from the Norwegian one, many feel attached to their Sami identity despite its low public status. In other Sami areas there has actually been a strong Sami revitalisation movement in recent years, proclaiming the virtues of Sami identity in a manner reminiscent of the 'Black is beautiful' movement in the United States.

Negotiating identity

An important insight from the Copperbelt studies, foreshadowed in Robert Park's 'urban ecology', was that ethnicity and social identities in general are relative and to some extent situational. As Mitchell writes, an individual can behave as a 'tribal' in some situations and as a 'town-dweller' in others (Mitchell, 1966). This fact should remind us that even in typical polyethnic societies where cultural differences are pervasive, there are many situations where ethnicity does not matter. This holds good not only in intraethnic relationships, but also in interethnic ones. Mauritian Hindus and Creoles often meet without implicitly or explicitly referring to their respective ethnic identities, for instance where the situation is defined through their statuses as colleagues or business partners.

The material from the Copperbelt and Mauritius also indicates that the compass of the 'We' category may expand and contract according to the situation. At general elections in Mauritius an individual may identify him or herself with the Hindu community at large; when looking for a job the extended kin group may be the relevant category, and when abroad he or she may actually take on an identity as simply Mauritian, even to the extent of feeling closer to Christian and Muslim Mauritians than to Hindus from India (Eriksen, 1992a: ch. 9). Similarly, Scandinavian identity is at its strongest when a Scandinavian encounters people from the neighbouring Scandinavian countries abroad. In most other situations that identity is not activated; it does not seem relevant in the definition of social situations. In other words, individuals have many statuses and many possible identities, and it is an empirical question when and how ethnic identities become the most relevant ones.

This fluidity and relativity of identity can sometimes be studied in interaction as negotiation of identity. *The Kalela Dance* exemplifies such a negotiation, where the agents disagree about the definition of their relationship. Mitchell describes the situation in this way:

A man and three women are drinking beer together in a beer-hall. One of the women belongs to the Lozi tribe. The man is a Ngoni, while the two other women are Ndebele. Suddenly the Lozi woman snatches a coin from him, says, 'A foreigner has lost his money,' and buys herself a cup of beer. The man asks why she took the money and demands that she give it back. She replies that there is a joking relationship between their tribes and that she was therefore entitled to take the money. The man denies that such a relationship exists. It then turns out that there is a joking relationship between the Lozi and the Ndebele, and that the woman identifies the man as being 'more or less' a Ndebele. The Ngoni and Ndebele tribes are linguistically and geographically close. The man insists that he is not a Ndebele but a Ngoni, but the woman does not pay him back. (Mitchell, 1956: 39-40)

In this situation, the Lozi woman insisted that a Ngoni was for practical purposes 'the same' as a Ndebele and could therefore be dealt with in the standardised way, whereas the man insisted that he was certainly not Ndebele. He challenged the validity of her taxonomic extension including the Ngoni in the same general category as the Ndebele. Similarly, London Brahmins might feel offended if they were to be treated, by native English people, in the same standardised way as black Britons of Jamaican origin. In such a situation the Brahmins would be challenging the English taxonomic category of 'immigrant', insisting that there were relevant differences between kinds of immigrants.

In other interethnic situations where identity is negotiated, the issue may rather be whether or not to make ethnic identity relevant. Although it may be difficult to neglect the ethnic dimension entirely in such situations, it can often effectively be over- or undercommunicated. Notably, members of stigmatised and powerless ethnic categories such as the coastal Sami would usually be prone to play down the importance of ethnicity in interaction with the dominant Norwegians – or they might try, in a negotiating approach, to present themselves as carriers of a Norwegian identity.

The point here is that ethnicity can be a fluid and ambiguous aspect of social life, and can to a considerable degree be manipulated by the agents themselves. Of course, ethnic identities cannot be manipulated indefinitely, and one cannot ascribe any identity to somebody by claiming, say, that an Irish person is 'really' a Jamaican. Ethnicity can be of varying importance in social situations, and it is often up to the agents themselves to decide upon its significance.

Ethnicity for the individual

When does ethnicity matter? It has already been stated that ethnicity occurs in social contexts where cultural differences 'make a difference'. But what kind of difference? This is a very complex question which we can only begin to explore here.

In the mining towns of the Copperbelt in the 1940s and 1950s, ethnicity played a small but not insignificant role in the allocation of jobs. Although workers were hired by the mining companies, people could use their ethnic networks as sources of information and recommendations when looking for work. Ethnic distinctions still had a part to play in matters pertaining to marriage. Mitchell (1956) and Epstein (1958; 1978) also report the modest emergence of what we would today call ethnopolitics, although ethnicity or 'tribalism' remained 'essentially a category of interaction in casual social intercourse' and did 'not form the basis for the organization of corporate groups' (Mitchell, 1956: 42). However, groups speaking the same language would, for example, protest that church services were conducted in a language unrelated to their own, and thus ethnic identity could function politically in certain contexts.

In Mauritius, which has a longer history as a plural society than the Copperbelt, ethnic membership can be important to individuals in a number of ways. Jobs have traditionally been allocated on an ethnic basis, usually through personal acquaintances or kinship. In many cases, religious associations and cults are also tightly linked with ethnic membership. Politics is thoroughly 'ethnified', and Mauritians tend to vote for parties which ostensibly represent the interests of their 'community'. Youth clubs tend to be ethnic or religious in character, and this is often where Mauritians make friends and meet prospective wives or husbands. Most families have traditionally insisted that their children marry within the 'community'. This means that in Mauritius ethnic membership can provide people with their livelihoods, their spouses, their friends and their religion.[2] In addition, ethnic

---

2 This description is particularly relevant for Mauritius before the 1980s, when the island went through a dramatic economic transformation, from a plantation society to an industrial one. Some consequences of these changes for ethnicity will be suggested in chapter 8.

identity offers a sense of continuity with the past and personal dignity. This aspect of ethnicity will be looked at more closely from chapter 4 onwards.

For ethnic membership to have a personal importance, it must provide the individual with something he or she considers valuable. However, we must make one important reservation: in some cases, ethnic identities are imposed from the outside, by dominant groups, on those who do not themselves want membership in the group to which they are assigned.

For many years, sociology and social anthropology contended that modernisation would eventually level out and remove ethnic distinctions. The general argument was that it would no longer be profitable to pay allegiance to ethnic groups in modern, individualistic and bureaucratic societies, and that the processes of modernisation would also remove the cultural differences between groups. This was Max Weber's view. Godfrey Wilson spoke of 'detribalisation', and in a later study of urbanisation in South Africa, Philip Mayer (1961) argued that 'trade unions transcend tribes', arguing along the same lines as Park, who described what he saw as melting-pot processes.

Do trade unions transcend tribes? Ethnicity has not only proved resilient in situations of change; it has also often emerged in forceful ways during the very processes of change which many believed would do away with it. On the other hand, there is no doubt that the meaning as well as the organisational form of ethnicity changes with other aspects of society. In order to find out what actually happens to ethnicity in the context of social change, we must therefore pose the question in more accurate terms than merely asking whether it disappears or stays the same.

What are the criteria for ethnicity?

Before we turn to look at ethnic group dynamics and processes of ethnic incorporation, we must enquire as to the substance of ethnic membership and classification. In other words, what is the stuff of ethnicity? How is it that some categories of people can be labelled ethnic while others cannot? Why is it that social classes, or the inhabitants of Somerset, or for that matter the members of a science-fiction association, are not considered ethnic groups, while the Sami, the Bisa and the Mauritian Creoles are? For a long time it was common to equate 'ethnic groups' with 'cultural groups'; any category of people who had 'a shared culture' was considered an ethnic group. As we have seen, this position has become difficult to justify. As Moerman discovered during fieldwork in Thailand (Moerman, 1965), the sharing of cultural traits frequently crosses group boundaries and, moreover, people do not always share all their 'cultural traits' with the same people. One may have the same language as some people, the same religion as some of those as well as of some others, and the same economic strategy as an altogether different category of people. In other words, cultural boundaries are not clear-cut, nor do they necessarily correspond with ethnic boundaries. As Eugeen Roosens remarks: 'There is more chance that the Flemish in Brussels, who always have to speak French, will become more "consciously" Flemish than their ethnic brothers and sisters in the rather isolated rural areas of West Flanders or Limburg' (Roosens, 1989: 12). With this observation, we are also reminded of the fact that ethnicity is an aspect of relationship, not a cultural property of a group. If a setting is wholly mono-ethnic, there is effectively no ethnicity, since there is nobody there to communicate cultural difference to.

It is also clear that the criteria which constitute ethnicity vary. It will simply not do to state that an ethnic group is marked by shared culture, or even to point at specific 'shared traits' such as shared religion, language and/or customs. The Mauritian case brings this out clearly. Of the four ethnic groups which legally exist in Mauritius, two are defined in relation to religion (Hindus and Muslims), one in relation to geographic origin (Chinese), and one is a residual category containing people with their origins in France, Africa and/or Madagascar (general population). Nearly all of the latter are Catholics, but this cannot be a distinguishing criterion since most of the Chinese are also Catholics. A few of those who are classified as Hindus are also Catholics.

Many anthropologists have grappled with the problem of criteria for what is and what is not ethnicity. Abner Cohen (1974b) has taken an extreme position in arguing that London stockbrokers may be said to constitute an ethnic group; they are largely endogamous (at least to the extent of marrying within their class) and have a shared identity. Many other anthropologists would wish to delimit ethnic status to groups with a more obvious permanence in time and a clearer cultural identity based on fictive kinship, and would perhaps emphasise that ethnic identity sticks to the individual, that one cannot entirely rid oneself of it (Barth, 1969a). The general problem remains, nevertheless: where should we draw the boundary between ethnic groups and other groups, such as social classes?

Manning Nash (1988) has proposed, as the lowest common denominators for all ethnic groups, the metaphors of 'bed, blood and cult'. By this he means that all ethnic groups consider themselves as biologically self-perpetuating and endogamous, that they have an ideology of shared ancestry, and that they have a shared religion. This kind of definition, whereby one denotes a number of so-called objective criteria for ethnicity, has been challenged on many occasions (see chapter 3). Nonetheless, ethnic groups or categories tend to have notions of common ancestry justifying their unity. But even this delineation can be problematic in practice, for how many generations does one have to go back in order to talk of shared ancestry?

Some ethnic groups use notions of 'race' or 'blood' in their ideology. Other groups rather use criteria of cultural competence. Some groups do not allow outsiders to assimilate, whereas others do. However, they all have notions of shared culture in common; in this ethnic groups are distinct from classes.

The main problems which have been posed here deal with the relationship between ethnicity and culture, and the question of where an ethnic group ends and another begins. We shall return to both of these questions regularly in later chapters.

This chapter has stressed that ethnicity is a product of contact and not of isolation, and it has also shown why the idea of an isolated ethnic group is meaningless. By implication, ethnicity entails both commonalities and differences between categories of people – both complementarisation and dichotomisation. The next chapter will show how social anthropologists conceptualise processes of ethnic incorporation and the maintenance of ethnic distinctions, or ethnic boundaries, through time.

3 THE SOCIAL ORGANISATION OF CULTURAL DISTINCTIVENESS

Cultural traits are not absolutes or simply intellectual categories, but are invoked to provide identities which legitimize claims to rights. They are strategies or weapons in competitions over scarce social goods.

Peter Worsley (1984: 249)

So far we have examined central aspects of interethnic processes, including stereotyping, under- and overcommunicating, dichotomisation and complementarisation, and ethnic stigma. In this chapter I shall go one step further and ask: how do ethnic groups develop, which ends do they serve and how are they reproduced through time? Although the emphasis remains on interpersonal ethnic processes involving acting individuals, it will also be stressed that ethnicity may be present in other, more encompassing, social contexts.

Ascription as a decisive feature of ethnicity

Towards the end of the last chapter, the question of the relationship between ethnicity and culture was posed. I noted that it would be misleading to state simply that ethnic groups are identical with cultural groups and that shared culture is the basis of ethnic identity. This problem has been raised by many anthropologists, and many of them have concluded that we should focus on social interaction and social organisation rather than 'cultural content'. Edmund Leach's famous monograph on the Kachin in Upper Burma (Leach, 1954) analyses the Kachin–Shan ethnic relationship. Leach argues that social organisation is more fundamental than culture:

Culture provides the form, the 'dress' of the social situation. As far as I am concerned, the cultural situation is a given factor, it is a product and an accident of history. I do not know *why* Kachin women go hatless with bobbed hair before they are married, but assume a turban afterwards, any more than I know *why* English women put on a ring on a particular finger to denote the same change in social status; all I am interested in is that in this Kachin context the assumption of a turban by a woman does have this symbolic significance. It is a statement about the [social] status of the woman. (Leach, 1954: 16)

In a later, very influential essay, Fredrik Barth (1969a) develops a model for the study of ethnic relations which conforms to Leach's general perspective in that it displaces 'culture' from the front stage of ethnic studies and argues that the focus of research ought to be the *boundaries* which delimit the group and not the 'cultural stuff' it encloses. Although it has clear predecessors in the Chicago School, in Leach's work, the Copperbelt studies and in less known contributions by Soviet scholars (cf. Bromley, 1974), Barth's essay was remarkable for its clarity and conciseness, and it has played a pivotal part in delineating the field of enquiry in the anthropological study of ethnicity.

Arguing against those anthropologists who identify ethnic groups with cultural units, Barth stresses that such definitions of ethnic groups 'allows us to assume that boundary maintenance is unproblematic and follows from the isolation which the itemized characteristics imply: racial difference, cultural difference, social separation and language barriers, spontaneous and organized enmity' (Barth, 1969a: 11). This, in his view, is unfortunate for two main reasons.

First, a focus on the cultural uniqueness of ethnic groups wrongly presupposes that groups tend to be isolated. On the contrary, Barth suggests, shared culture may profitably be seen as an implication or result of a long-term social process, rather than as a primordial feature of groups.

Second, definitions based on notions of shared culture wrongly imply that the maintenance of ethnic boundaries is unproblematic. In fact, Barth argues, the main task for the anthropological study of ethnicity consists in accounting for the maintenance and consequences of ethnic boundaries. As groups are in continuous contact with one another, the persistent fact of cultural variation requires to be accounted for, since this is not a fact of nature.

This approach to ethnicity advocates a focus on that which is *socially effective* in interethnic relations, and Barth regards the ethnic group chiefly in terms of social organisation. It follows that ethnic groups must be defined from within, from the perspective of their members. Instead of listing traits of 'objective culture', which members often share with non-members anyway, Barth defines ethnicity as categorical ascriptions which classify individuals in terms of their 'basic, most general identity'. Since ethnic membership must be acknowledged by the agents themselves in order to be socially effective, this is the crucial criterion for Barth. As he notes, it 'makes no difference how dissimilar members may be in their overt behaviour – if they say they are A, in contrast to another cognate category B, ... they declare their allegiance to the shared culture of A's' (Barth, 1969a: 15). The discontinuity between ethnic groups is chiefly a social discontinuity, not a cultural one.

A different position would hold that ethnic identities and boundaries ought to be studied in relation to large-scale historical processes which the agents themselves can only influence to a negligible extent (see chapter 5). For now, we shall focus on the kinds of insight into ethnic processes which may emerge from a focus on ethnic boundaries.

Boundary maintenance

In stressing that the focus of investigation ought to be the boundary that separates the ethnic groups from each other, Barth advocates a *relational* and *processual* approach to ethnicity. The ethnic group is defined through its relationship to others, highlighted through the boundary, and the boundary itself is a social product which may have variable importance and which may change through time. The group's culture as well as forms of social organisation may change without removing the ethnic boundary. In some cases, groups may actually become culturally more similar at the same time that boundaries are strengthened. This, it could be argued, has been the case in Trinidad, where a cultural 'Creolisation' of the population of Indian descent has taken place during the same period as a strong ethnic revitalisation and emphasis on boundary maintenance (Vertovec, 1992; Eriksen, 1992b; see also chapter 5). Conversely, Jan-Petter Blom (1969) has shown that, due to peculiar ecological circumstances, Norwegian mountain farmers lead a very different life from lowland farmers, yet they are not considered a distinct ethnic group. It would therefore be misleading to argue that ethnic boundaries contain 'cultures'. Cultural differences relate to ethnicity if and only if such differences are made relevant in social interaction.

The outbreak of civil war in Yugoslavia in 1991, and the eventual fragmentation of the federation, exemplifies the relativity of ethnic boundaries. There had been peace between Serbs and Croats since 1945, and the rate of intermarriage between the groups had been high. Serbs and Croats speak the same language. Perhaps the main cultural differences between the groups are that they practise different variants of Christianity and that they use different scripts (the Serbs are Orthodox and use the Cyrillic alphabet, while the Croats are Catholic and use Latin script). Nonetheless, it was repeatedly stressed, following the outbreak of the war in June 1991, that the groups were irreconcilable and culturally incompatible; Serbs claimed that the Croats were fascists, and Croats claimed that the Serbs were imperialists.[1] Ethnic boundaries, dormant for decades, were activated; presumed cultural differences which had been irrelevant for two generations were suddenly 'remembered' and invoked as proof that it was impossible for the two groups to live side by side. It is only when they *make a difference* in interaction that cultural differences are important in the creation of ethnic boundaries.

Barth further argues that cultural variation may indeed be an *effect* and not a *cause* of boundaries. If the mutual dichotomisation between Serbs and Croats continues and the national borders between their states become permanent, it is likely that their languages as well as other aspects of culture will gradually become more distinctive.

Boundary transcendence

Ethnic boundaries are not necessarily territorial boundaries, but social ones. They do not isolate groups entirely from each other; rather, there is a continuous flow of information, interaction, exchange and sometimes even people across them. The latter point needs to be exemplified, since it is normally assumed that people do not change ethnic membership.

An example cited by Barth is the flow of people across the Pathan–Baluch boundary in north-western Pakistan. Because of differences between the respective political systems, a male Pathan who has lost his position in Pathan society can be assimilated with his entire household as a client of a Baluch chief. Although clientship is despised among Pathans, it can be honourable enough among the Baluch. This change of identity is naturally two-sided: in assuming Baluch identity, one loses Pathan identity even if one's Pathan origins remain acknowledged. In this way, the boundaries are maintained despite a flow of personnel across them.

---

1 Gellner (1983) has written that the religious labels distinguishing the ethnic groups in polyethnic Bosnia refer to past, not present differences. 'What [the Bosnian Muslims] meant was that they could not describe themselves as Serb or as Croat (despite sharing a language with Serbs and Croats), because these identifications carried the implications of *having been* Orthodox or Catholic ... Nowadays, to be a Bosnian Muslim you need not believe that there is no God but God and that Mohamed is his Prophet, but you do need to have lost that faith' (Gellner, 1983: 71–2)

Gunnar Haaland (1969) describes the mechanisms of boundary tran-
scendence in Darfur, western Sudan. Haaland describes the
relationship between two groups, the Fur, who are sedentary culti-
vators, and the Baggara, who are pastoral nomads. Although they have
been in contact for centuries, the two groups differ 'with regard to
general style of life, subsistence pattern, overt cultural features like
language, house type and weapons, and standards for evaluation of
performance' (Haaland, 1969: 59). The ethnic boundary between the
groups seems a rather impermeable one. Unlike the situation of the
Lue and their neighbours, the ethnic segments of Chicago or the relationship between the tribal categories on the Copperbelt, the
boundaries between the Fur and the Baggara are highly visible and
are closely related to distinct cultural practices. Yet there are many
examples of people who cross the boundary permanently.

The relationship between Fur and Baggara can be described as one
based on economic complementarity. They exchange goods; notably,
the Fur sell millet and receive milk and livestock in return. There is
also some exchange of services between the groups. There is a clear
dichotomisation of identities in interaction. The main reason that
some Fur still choose to become Baggara, argues Haaland, is economic.
For although Fur are chiefly growers of millet, many also own cows.
When a Fur farming family has a certain number of cows, it is no longer
profitable for it to remain sedentary. The family would then allocate
its resources more efficiently by shifting to a semi-nomadic way of
life. Such a shift is only the first step in the process of identity change.
After a certain period of semi-nomadism when the household still
cultivates some millet and stays close to the Fur village, it will
eventually have a sufficient number of cattle to migrate to distant
Baggara areas during the rainy season, and will no longer depend on
millet cultivation. Then the household will attach itself to a camp of
Arabic-speaking Baggara. The children will grow up speaking Arabic
and will not learn the categories of Fur culture. They will consider
themselves, and will be considered as, Baggara; 'they will constitute
disappearing lines in local Fur genealogies' (Haaland, 1969: 65).
Moreover, in interaction with sedentary Fur they will be treated as
Baggara, since the same standardised statuses will be made relevant
in the market-place and other arenas for interethnic encounters.
Despite the fact that about 1 per cent of the Fur turn nomadic every
year, the boundaries between the groups remain intact.

The rationale for the crossing of boundaries is in this case clearly
economic. Nomadisation would therefore probably stop in Darfur,
since new investment opportunities were emerging for the sedentary
population in the 1960s. Could this be stated as a general principle?

Not unless we define 'economic' in a very wide sense, including non-tangible benefits. For a member of a stigmatised ethnic group, it may be worthwhile to assimilate even if it does not pay off economically, so long as it removes the stigma. Studies of caste-climbing in India (Bailey, 1968) have thus shown that low castes may be willing to invest considerable amounts of money in order to achieve a higher ritual status, and similar processes take place with ethnic groups. It should also be remembered that identity change is not always possible. Blacks in the United States, for example, cannot choose to become white, even if they spend several generations, or great sums of money on cosmetic surgery, on the attempt. In this regard, the boundaries between whites and blacks are more rigid than the boundaries between Fur and Baggara.

Degrees of ethnic incorporation

The concept of ethnic boundary places the focus of ethnic studies on the *relationship* between groups. The boundary is that invisible dividing line *between* them. Boundaries are generally two-way; that is to say, both groups in a relationship demarcate their identity and distinctiveness vis-à-vis the other. Concerning the character of the groups that the boundaries contain, Barth mentions their variable social importance. At one extreme, ethnicity can function merely as categorical ascriptions or labels used to classify people, which was to a great extent the case in the Copperbelt. At the other extreme, ethnic organisation may organise crucial aspects of the individual's life and have great importance at the level of society. As Abner Cohen has argued:

There is ethnicity and ethnicity ... I think that it is common sense that the ethnicity of a collectivity that manifests itself in the form of an annual gathering of a few of its numbers to perform a dance or a ceremonial is different from the ethnicity manifested by, say, the Catholics in Northern Ireland. (A. Cohen, 1974a: xiv)

This variability in the organisational importance of ethnicity has been explored by Don Handelman (1977), who has constructed a useful typology of degrees of ethnic incorporation – from the very loose and socially almost insignificant category to the tight corporate group. He distinguishes between the ethnic category, the ethnic network, the ethnic association and the ethnic community. I will now show how this typology may shed light on ethnicity in Mauritius.

The least incorporated kind of ethnic collectivity is the *ethnic category*, which provides its members little in terms of tangible valuables. The ethnic category is constituted by the fact that contrastive categories are used to identify members and outsiders; its shared 'assets' could be described as 'categorical corporate holdings' (Handelman, 1977: 264). In other words, ethnic category membership teaches the individual appropriate behaviour vis-à-vis others, passes on knowledge about his or her (imputed) origins, and legitimises the existence of the ethnic category. In a system of interaction where corporate ethnic groups do not exist, but where ethnic categorisation is used, ethnicity may still be highly important as a guiding principle for interaction. In Mauritius, the Creoles may be said to be an ethnic category (Eriksen, 1986; 1988). They consider themselves, and are considered by others, as culturally distinctive. Yet they are politically fragmented and lack overarching organisations as well as effective interpersonal networks based on ethnicity.

The next degree of ethnic incorporation in Handelman's typology is the *ethnic network*. This concept 'suggests that people will regularly interact with one another in terms of an ethnic membership set' (Handelman, 1977: 269). Such a network, while based on principles of ethnic categorisation, creates enduring interpersonal ties between members of the same category and can also serve to organise contacts between strangers. The main difference between categories and networks consists in the latter's ability to distribute resources among group members. In situations where members of one's own group are preferred in the job market, ethnic networks are activated. However, the ethnic network is decentralised and can be broken down into dyadic relationships: it has no organisational nexus. In Mauritius, the Franco-Mauritians may be said to constitute an ethnic network. As they are a small numerical minority in a parliamentary democracy, they lack shared political organisation and do not function as a visible interest group, but there remains a strong sense of solidarity and cultural uniqueness. There are strong moral obligations for Franco-Mauritians to support each other on an individual basis.[2]

The ethnic category is constituted through the consistent application of mutually exclusive identity labels, and the ethnic network additionally channels a great deal of interaction along ethnic lines. When members of an ethnic category feel that they have shared interests, and develop an organisational apparatus to express them, it would be appropriate to talk of an *ethnic association*. Although

---

2 During fieldwork in Mauritius, I have often been mistaken for a Franco-Mauritian. Once, when a Franco-Mauritian gave me a lift while I was hitch-hiking, he remarked on Franco solidarity, adding that he would probably not have stopped had he known I was foreign.

Handelman describes this as a political pressure group encompassing only its members, one may usefully extend the notion to include ethnic categories where a larger or smaller segment of the members is active in such an organisation. The ethnic association, then, embodies the presumed shared interests of the ethnic category at a collective, corporative level. Mauritian Hindus may be mentioned as an example of an ethnic category incorporated in ethnic associations, which articulate the group's collective goals at the level of national society. Such organisations may be political parties, but they may also be Hindu youth clubs (*baitkas*) or religious associations.

The highest degree of ethnic incorporation is that of the *ethnic community*. This kind of collectivity has, in addition to ethnic networks and shared political organisation, a territory with more or less permanent physical boundaries. Ethnic groups in political command of nation-states are eminent examples of ethnic communities in this meaning of the word. In a multi-ethnic island-state like Mauritius, no territorially located ethnic community exists, although the Sino-Mauritians or Chinese are close to meeting the requirements. They are linked through tight social networks based on kinship, affinity and friendship, and have pooled considerable economic and political resources in ethnic associations. About half of the category of 30,000 live in a clearly demarcated quarter, Chinatown, in Port-Louis. Handelman's main point, which is only partly true with respect to the Sino-Mauritians, is that the territorially based ethnic organisation places additional demands on its members: they are collectively responsible for guarding the boundaries and for ensuring the continued control of the territory.

As Figure 3.1 indicates, ethnic categorisation is logically prior to the other forms of incorporation.

Handelman's typology can be read in a number of ways. It can be seen, as he suggests himself, as a *developmental framework* useful for the analysis of ethnogenesis or the emergence of ethnic corporate groups out of categories. There seems to be a clear development in time from the category through the network and the association to the community. It can nevertheless also be viewed, as my Mauritian examples suggest, as a non-developmental *typology of ethnic organisation*, where different types may coexist within the same polyethnic society. Finally, the typology may be interpreted as a model of *aspects of interethnic processes*. Thus one may through the course of a day pass from a situation where only one's categorical ascription is relevant, to a situation where one's ethnic network is activated, and later to situations where one's ethnic category appears as an association or an ethnic community. Even the Mauritian Creoles, who are usually

	Category	Network	Association	Community
Standardised ethnic ascriptions	X	X	X	X
Interaction along ethnic lines		X	X	X
Goal-oriented corporate organisation			X	X
Territorial base				X
e.g. in Mauritius	*Creoles*	*Franco-M*	*Hindus*	*Sino-M*

Figure 3.1: Degrees of ethnic incorporation

Source: after Handelman, 1977.

a fragmented ethnic category lacking leadership and corporate organisation, have occasionally existed as an ethnic association. This has notably come about during election campaigns with politicians overtly representing Creole interests.

If Handelman's typology is read as an evolutionary schema, it should be kept in mind that not all ethnic categories undergo these transitions. In many cases, a very real alternative to ethnic incorporation can be assimilation. A great number of ethnic categories or groups have disappeared from the face of the earth in this way.

In a comparison between Hausa in Ibadan and Luo in Kampala, David Parkin (1974) makes a distinction which is similar to Handelman's typology. Parkin's main argument is that ethnicity is likely to take on corporative characteristics if a group is (i) economically self-sufficient, (ii) residentially segregated, (iii) insulated from the dominant values of greater society, and/or (iv) occupationally specialised (Parkin, 1974: 126–7). Parkin's distinction between 'interpersonal' and 'congregational' ethnicity also resembles the common distinction between 'private' and 'public' fields of interaction. Everything else being equal, an ethnic group operating in a public field will be more tightly integrated than one confined to private fields.

Such typologies of ethnic incorporation deal with ethnicity as a kind of social organisation, and they exemplify Barth's general point that the social content of ethnicity is highly variable. Seen from the individual actor's point of view, the main variable in the typology consists in the constraints and opportunities, or rights and duties, offered by ethnicity. However, the typology may also indicate circumstances under which ethnicity becomes a particularly important aspect of personal identity. It is evident that ethnic identity is normally more important to a member of an ethnic community than to a member of an ethnic category.

Ethnicity as resource competition

Abner Cohen's perspective on ethnicity, which is related to Barth's,[3] defines ethnic organisation essentially as a kind of political organisation. In Cohen's view, social interaction and organisation are essentially dual phenomena: they comprise aspects of utility and aspects of meaning. 'Political man is also symbolic man' (A. Cohen, 1974b: Preface). Ethnicity, he argues, is an organisational form which exploits this duality for particular ends, which may or may not be acknowledged by the agents themselves. Ethnic ideology has an immediate appeal because it offers answers to 'the perennial problems of life': the questions of origins, destiny and, ultimately, the meaning of life. However, Cohen argues, ethnicity must also have a practical function in order to be viable. Only by focusing on this aspect is it possible to explain why some ethnic groups thrive while others vanish, and why only some ethnic identifications assume great social importance. Two empirical studies by Cohen exemplify this approach (A. Cohen, 1969; 1981). Both depict ethnicity as an instrument for competition over scarce resources, which is nevertheless circumscribed by ideologies of shared culture, shared origins and metaphoric kinship.

The earlier of these monographs analyses the organisation of Hausa trade networks in the Yoruba city of Ibadan, western Nigeria (A. Cohen, 1969). Hausa migrants to Ibadan succeeded, in a relatively short space of time, in virtually monopolising cattle trade in the city. This was accomplished by way of ethnic organisation. Cattle was bought from Hausa traders in northern Nigeria. Consciously drawing on ethnic solidarity expressed in the idiom of shared culture, and strengthening their group cohesion by joining the orthodox Muslim

3 However, Cohen has argued against what he sees as Barth's subjectivism (A. Cohen, 1974a; 1974b).

Tijaniyya order, the Hausa in Ibadan quickly established reliable trade links with the north. In Cohen's analysis, this was a principal function of ethnicity. Had it not been profitable to be a Hausa in Ibadan and to communicate one's ethnic identity to other Hausas and thereby strengthen ethnic boundaries, Hausa identity might well have disappeared in the Yoruba city.

The second monograph (A. Cohen, 1981) analyses the ways in which Creole[4] political interests were expressed in Sierra Leone during a period when ethnic politics were officially illegitimate. The Creoles were a professional elite, and the political elite, dominated by the numerically superiour Temne and Mende, aimed at reducing their dominance in white-collar professions. Cohen shows how the Creoles succeeded in retaining their privileges through becoming freemasons on a large scale and turning the Masonic lodges into unofficial Creole associations. Although the linkages thus developed might be described as ethnic networks rather than an ethnic association, the group succeeded in reproducing its boundaries and in keeping its 'corporate holdings' within the group. Information about available jobs, scholarships and so on was passed on inside the Masonic network, and the symbolic capital of the ethnic category was thereby kept inside the boundary. As in the Hausa monograph, Cohen argues that the identity tag 'Creole' would have been much less important (and might have vanished) if Creoledom did not have a clear function for its members.

Levels of ethnicity

Most of the anthropologists who have written about ethnic organisation have seen it in the context of competition for scarce resources. The focus has been on organisational forms reminiscent of Handelman's associations and communities rather than categories and networks. Many have seen ethnicity plainly as a possible instrument for pursuing particular interests, or for maximising values. In a book on contemporary ethnopolitics, Roosens (1989: 13) states that '[m]any people change their ethnic identity only if they can profit by doing so'.

---

4 The term 'Creole' is not an analytic concept. In Mauritius 'Creole' refers to people of largely African descent. In Sierra Leone it means people who are acknowledged to be descendants of liberated slaves. They are contrasted with 'tribals'. In Trinidad 'Creole' means any Trinidadian of non-East Indian descent (which could be European, African, Chinese, Lebanese/Syrian or mixed), and in the French *département* of La Réunion *créole* refers chiefly to whites born in the island.

There are two common criticisms of this kind of perspective. First, it pays little attention to the symbolic aspect of ethnicity, ethnic identity, treating it either as irrelevant or as contingent on utility (see chapter 4). Second, through a focus on competition and interpersonal relationships, one will often fail to account for power differences in the society in question, even when this is important as a context for the competition.

A focus on power relations may nevertheless divert attention from other important issues. In the Copperbelt, for example, there was scarcely any ethnically based division of labour (provided we exclude the few whites in the area, which the researchers did!). The relationships between the African groups could in this respect be described as *symmetrical*; they took part in the same social system in roughly the same way. When there is an ethnic division of labour, a different pattern of ethnicity results. Very often, ethnicity then takes on a more strongly *hierarchical* character, where the groups are ranked according to their differential access to resources, and here the correlation between class and ethnicity is high.

In a study of ethnic resource competition in Guyana, Leo Despres (1975a) tries to integrate an analysis of societal power relations with an analysis of interpersonal ethnicity by distinguishing between three societal levels where ethnicity is articulated.

Guyanese society is polyethnic. The bulk of the population is divided between Africans (descendants of slaves) and East Indians (descendants of indentured labourers). At the 'level of the overall social system', that of Guyanese society as a whole, the economy is dominated by foreign interests. There is also an ethnic division of labour. The Indians tend to be rural and work in agriculture or small businesses, whereas most of the Africans are urban and do non-agricultural work. The Indians are more numerous than the Africans and have a higher birth rate, but the government is African-dominated. Thus the civil service also tends to be African-dominated. Since ethnicity functions as an ordering principle in interaction, competition for available resources 'has served to order categorically identified elements [ethnic categories] of the Guyanese population in an arrangement of unequal status and power' (Despres, 1975a: 99). This is a clear macro perspective, delineating the conditions, or structural parameters, for interethnic relations at the interpersonal level.

At the second level, that of 'organised ethnic group relations' (Handelman's 'associations' or Parkin's 'congregations'), Despres mentions a large number of organisations which more or less overtly represent the interest of a particular ethnic group. On the one hand, he describes how ethnic leaders pursue group political interests within organisations ostensibly devoted to religion or 'culture'; on the other, he describes the struggle for control over unions and parastatal bodies as interethnic competition. At this level, the ethnic categories themselves appear as corporate actors. Indians and Africans alike identify themselves with 'their own' leaders. Political parties are strongly ethnically based in Guyana, as in several other polyethnic countries. Ethnic differences, in other words, seem more important than other kinds of political differences.

The third level singled out by Despres is that of 'interpersonal encounters'. At this level, he finds much of that ambiguity, relativity and negotiation which was described in chapter 2. He finds many instances of dichotomisation (the creation of Us–Them contrasts) and notes that many informal social groupings are mono-ethnic. But he also stresses that Guyanese are flexible in switching situationally between identities. In interethnic situations, the typical mode of complementarisation (the creation of We–You relationships) stresses *equality*. The nation-building ideology of independent Guyana stresses the irrelevance of ethnicity in relation to citizenship. Despres also notes that in relation to foreigners, people tend to take on an identity as Guyanese (in contrast to Trinidadian, Jamaican, American, or whatever) rather than as Africans or East Indians. Since ethnic identities are situationally defined, they are imperative only under particular circumstances. In a society like Guyana, where ethnic incorporation is discouraged by the state and where there is great social tension between the groups (there have been numerous 'race riots' since the 1950s), it makes sense that ethnicity should be undercommunicated in daily interethnic encounters.

A main theoretical point in Despres' analysis is that in order to understand ethnicity at the interpersonal level it is necessary to know something about the societal conditions which structure interethnic encounters. Although this perspective incorporates Barth's emphasis on the ethnic group as an organisational vessel based on subjective self-ascription, it introduces an additional element in the account of ethnicity, namely the institutional framework of society. Before considering the relationship between social class and ethnicity, I shall present a perspective on polyethnic societies whose focus is almost entirely on the institutional arrangements of society.

The theory of plural societies

The theory of plural societies may be compatible with the Barthian model of ethnic differentiation and boundary maintenance, but it does not focus on the acting individual or on the competitive advantages of ethnic organisation. Rather, it deals with the *integration of societies* and is historically linked with the tradition from Durkheim and Radcliffe-Brown in social anthropology: that is, structural-functionalism.

The theory of pluralism is usually associated with J.S. Furnivall, who wrote extensively on the Dutch and British colonies of South-East Asia (Furnivall, 1948). He regarded these 'plural' societies as being composed of groups which were socially and culturally discrete, which were integrated through economic symbiosis (or mutual interdependence) and the political domination of one group (the colonial masters), but which were otherwise socially discrete, as well as being distinctive concerning language, religion and customs. There were no shared values in these societies, argued Furnivall, and so the groups were held together in a political system by the coercive force of the state, the police and the military. Such societies were in his view deeply divided.

A leading contemporary interpreter of pluralist theory is M.G. Smith. His principal work deals with the West Indies before and immediately after independence (M.G. Smith, 1965; 1984). Smith has defined his unit of study as 'the plural society as a unit of disparate parts which owes its existence to external factors, and lacks a common social will' (M.G. Smith, 1965: vii). In a typical plural society, the constituent groups will be differentially integrated: there will be a wide array of ethnically discrete fields of activity, so that extensive contact and mutual influence are kept at a low level. In Smith's view, plural societies are notoriously unstable precisely because they lack 'a common social will'.

Although Smith has been severely criticised for regarding ethnic groups as static as well as for reifying culture (seeing cultures as fixed and closed systems), notions similar to Smith's are implicit in many studies of ethnicity. If the focus of the investigation is on the ethnic boundary that keeps ethnic groups discrete, then one is led to regard the total system as a 'unit of disparate parts', even if the analysis focuses on the contact between members of different ethnic categories. How much contact across ethnic boundaries is necessary for a society to cease to be a volatile plural society composed of discrete groups with no shared values? Conversely, one might say that virtually every society is a unit of disparate parts in so far as it consists of competing interest groups (Jenkins, 1986).

The theory of social and cultural pluralism is a clear example of what can be called an objectivist approach in ethnicity studies. According to Smith, a chief cause of ethnic differentiation is objective differences of culture. Whereas Barth sees cultural differentiation as a long-term effect of ethnic differentiation and Cohen would regard the cultural aspect of ethnicity as subordinate to its social functioning, Smith sees culture largely as an independent variable. According to this view, ethnicity and ethnic identity cannot be chosen, situationally or otherwise, since there is an intrinsic link between ethnicity and language, custom and social organisation. Since cultural discontinuity is a readily observable fact, this perspective may represent a challenge to ethnicity studies, which have largely been concerned with the social organisational and political aspects of ethnicity while disregarding the cultural dimension (cf. Bentley, 1987; Eriksen, 1991a; Haaland, 1992). In later chapters, we shall pursue some of the difficult questions concerning the relationship between ethnicity and culture further.

Ethnicity and rank

Some writers distinguish between 'ranked' and 'unranked' polyethnic systems (for example, Horowitz, 1985). This distinction suggests that in some societies, ethnic groups compete for scarce resources on an equal footing, whereas others are based on systematically unequal access to resources. From an anthropological point of view, such a distinction is unfortunate because it classifies entire societies on the basis of a single principle which is far from unambiguous. Therefore, it may be a better solution to assume that ethnicity may, in different contexts in societies, appear as either horizontal or vertical aspects of social classification. If we regard ethnicity in its horizontal aspect, it may be relevant to focus on competition for scarce resources and/or processes of dichotomisation and boundary maintenance. If, on the other hand, we focus on the vertical aspects of ethnicity, it will be more relevant to focus on power relations. Both the vertical and the horizontal aspects of ethnicity vary in importance: situationally, historically and between societies.

Ethnic ideologies may justify social hierarchies. It is therefore necessary to clarify the relationship between ethnicity and other criteria for hierarchisation. There is never a simple one-to-one relationship between ethnic membership and rank in a society. The reason is that there are always additional criteria for rank. Gender, class membership, age and other criteria – which vary from society to society – all contribute to defining a person's rank. To illustrate this complexity, we may ask who has the highest rank in British society: a female black surgeon or a male white gardener? It would not be possible to arrive at a simple, unambiguous answer to this question.

In many polyethnic societies, there is nevertheless a high *correlation* between ethnic identity and class membership. In colonial plantation societies (in the Caribbean, in South America and elsewhere), the division of labour was strongly correlated with ethnic identifications; in industrial European societies, non-European immigrants generally occupy the lowest-ranking jobs. It must nevertheless be emphasised that although ethnicity and class may be linked, they refer to different categorisations. Even in clearly ethnically ranked societies, like South Africa and Namibia during apartheid, there are great variations in class membership within any ethnic categories – there are black capitalists as well as white manual workers.

'Doxic' stereotyping ('doxa' is Bourdieu's, 1977, term for the unquestionable, taken-for-granted aspects of culture) is very powerful in many polyethnic societies and can often function as self-fulfilling prophecies: the negative stereotype created by a dominant group may become part of a group's view of itself. Such stereotyping in turn usually feeds on differences in the respective positions of ethnic groups in the economy and the political system. Peter Worsley (1984: 236) thus notes that 'whole peoples ... are perceived as being naturally suited for distinctive roles in the division of labour, and these "natural" differences often include cultural as well as physical characteristics'.

Worsley further criticises those theorists who assume that there is an 'invariant relationship' between the two criteria for social differentiation; that is, that ethnic groups tend to be congruent with classes in polyethnic class societies. Rather, he continues, class divisions may be related to ethnic divisions in three main ways:

They may *overlap*, reinforcing each other in a congruent or isomorphic manner (as when all workers in a given factory, industry, town or region are of the same ethnic background). If the employer is of a different ethnic background, this solidarity is further reinforced. Ethnicity may, however, cut *across* class, vertically, when members of the same ethnic group are to be found at various levels as workers, clerks or managers, and the employer may also be of the same ethnic group. Thirdly, classes may be *segmented* by ethnicity with skilled workers drawn from one ethnic group, unskilled from another, and so forth: one segment may be of the same ethnic affiliation as management; others may not. (Worsley, 1984: 240)

In Mauritian society, all three kinds of relationship between ethnicity and class can be identified. The mutually reinforcing and localised variety can be found in some coastal villages where the majority of inhabitants are Creoles engaged in fishing, and in some agricultural villages where the majority of the population are Hindu smallholders, labourers or sharecroppers.

Worsley's second type, where ethnicity cuts across class, can be observed in Mauritian towns and in the textile industry, the bureaucracy and in tourism. Members of most ethnic groups may be found at most class levels, although they are not equally represented at each level.

The third variety, perhaps most characteristic of colonial Mauritian society (before 1968), can still be identified in the many villages associated with the large sugar estates. The estates themselves are owned by Franco-Mauritians. The Creoles of these villages tend to work at the factory as skilled workers, whereas the Hindus and Muslims tend to be field labourers. In these villages there is often a single grocery which is run by a Sino-Mauritian family. In some of them there is virtually a one-to-one relationship between ethnic membership and occupation.

Folk taxonomies tend to link ethnic categorisation with occupational categories as well as 'cultural traits'. In a study of the relationship between ethnicity and class in highland Peru, Pierre van den Berghe states:

Ethnicity and class are interrelated but *analytically distinct* phenomena. The fact that different social classes most commonly show subcultural differences and, conversely, that ethnic groups living under a common government are more often than not ordered in a hierarchy of power, wealth and status does not make class reducible to ethnicity, or ethnicity to class. (van den Berghe, 1975: 73)

The main social hierarchies in Peru can be described as several partly overlapping systems of domination. In geographic terms, the countryside is dominated by the town, the town by the regional centre, the regional centre by the capital city and the capital by international metropolises. The class system, the administrative or political hierarchy and the linguistic hierarchies are similarly constituted as relationships of domination. Finally, in the ethnic hierarchy, the Mestizos (mixed Indian–European descent) dominate the *cholos* (mixed Mestizo–Indian descent), who in turn dominate the Indians. (There are few Peruvians of European descent.) There is a high correlation between ethnic membership, area of residence, education and linguistic abilities, and class membership. At one end of the continuum there is the cosmopolitan elite, and a typical member of this group is a Mestizo who is trilingual in Spanish, English and French, university-educated, lives in Lima and is a member of a wealthy family with business interests. At the other end of the continuum we find the marginal peasants, who are Indians, largely monolingual in one of the low-status languages (Quechua or Aymara), illiterate and propertyless.

The interrelationship between criteria

Despite this high correlation between class membership and ethnic membership, van den Berghe emphasises that the two principles for differentiation function in different ways and ought to be distinguished from each other analytically. He outlines two typical kinds of situation marked by different relationships between class and ethnicity. The first is the colonial African variety, where, to use Worsley's term, the social classes are 'segmented' by ethnicity. Movement of individuals across the ethnic boundaries, which are highly correlated with class and are often codified as 'race', is extremely difficult, although considerable cultural assimilation may take place.

In the other kind of situation, of which Peru is a characteristic example, the 'ethnic groups are clearly hierarchical, but the culturally dominant group is relatively open to members of other ethnic groups' (van den Berghe, 1975: 78). Movement across the ethnic boundary is possible, provided the people in question succeed in acquiring cultural characteristics and class membership associated with the higher-ranking ethnic category. (Downward mobility along these lines is also possible.) Many individuals are ethnically ambiguous; indeed, the largest ethnic category in highland Peru, the *cholo* category, is seen as a fuzzy intermediate category between the 'poles' of Mestizo and Indian. Designation of *cholo*-ness is largely situational in that Mestizos tend to describe their social inferiors as *cholos*. The inhabitants of a highland town would be *cholos* seen from Lima, but they would be regarded as Mestizos from the perspective of the countryside, by virtue of their urban way of life, their dress code and so on. Despite this social transference of class characteristics to ethnic classifications and the high correlation between the two criteria for differentiation, it would be misleading to claim that there is a one-to-one relationship between class and ethnicity. Although class membership is partly determined by a person's command of languages and acquisition of particular cultural markers, class is also determined by several non-ethnic factors. Conversely, there are many aspects of ethnic identity and boundary maintenance which are unrelated to class.

The example from Peru nevertheless shows that there is a certain *contagious* effect of class on ethnicity and vice versa. Etienne Balibar (1991), writing about 'class racism', has argued that ethnic discrimination in France derives from a widely held assumption to the effect that classes are 'natural', and that the idea of superior and inferior races has replaced the aristocratic–commoner dichotomy in French society. As my own work indicates (Eriksen, 1986; 1988), a Mauritian Creole who becomes a member of the middle class and thereby acquires Coloured ethnic characteristics, may change ethnic membership and effectively *become* a Coloured or *gen de couleur*. Further, as M.G. Smith (1965) has noted for the West Indies, people in this kind of society often believe that they classify others by virtue of skin colour, whereas the actual classification relates to class or other criteria of socio-economic status.

Many light-skinned Mauritians are classified as Creoles or *ti-kreol* ('small Creoles'), since they live in a way considered typical of Creoles – they are manual workers or fisherfolk, poor and have many children. Similarly, many dark-skinned Mauritians are considered *gens de couleur* by virtue of their education, use of French language at home and middle-class suburban place of residence. Actual colour is not unimportant in social classification (successful male Creoles tend to marry women with lighter skins than themselves), but in practical classification it functions together with other criteria.

It is widely seen as 'unnatural' that a Franco-Mauritian should be poor or that a Creole should be rich. In the case of one poor Franco-Mauritian in a Mauritian town, some of his acquaintances argued that he was 'really' a Mulatto – they claimed that there were 'negroes' in his ancestry. However, although the relationship between class and ethnicity is sometimes evident and although ethnic classification is sometimes contingent on class membership, we should keep in mind that the relationship varies between societies, and also within societies. Although 'Creole' connotes working class in Mauritius, there are people who are acknowledged as, and regard themselves as Creoles, who belong to the middle class.

Some controversies

Disagreements between anthropologists who study ethnicity sometimes reflect fundamental theoretical differences. At this stage some such disagreements will only be outlined, and I shall return to them later.

First, it can be instructive to distinguish between 'primordialist' and 'instrumentalist' perspectives on ethnicity. Barth describes ethnic categories as 'organisational vessels that may be given varying amounts and forms of content in different sociocultural systems' (Barth, 1969a: 14). Implicitly, he seems to say that despite the contact across boundaries and the change in cultural content of the groups, the ethnic categories as such are constants which may be called upon when the need arises, as in a competitive situation. Barth explicitly defines ethnic ascriptions as categorical ascriptions which classify 'a person in terms of his basic, most general identity, presumptively determined by his origin and background' (1969a: 13). Abner Cohen has argued against this view, which he sees as a 'primordialist' position since it defines ethnic identity as an imperative status, as a more or less immutable aspect of the social person. Although Barth argued forcefully against cultural determinism in ethnic studies and stressed the need for investigating the social enactment of ethnicity through flexible and negotiable boundary processes, Cohen accuses him of promoting a static view on ethnicity (A. Cohen, 1974a: xii–xv). In Cohen's view, ethnic identities develop in response to functional organisational requirements. He defines ethnicity simply as a particular form of informal political organisation where cultural boundaries are invoked so that the group's resources or 'symbolic capital' can be secured. In this way, Cohen goes even further than Barth in severing the tie between ethnicity and culture. Indeed, as mentioned above, he regards London stockbrokers as an ethnic group (A. Cohen, 1974a; 1974b).

Cohen's reorientation both widens and narrows the scope of ethnic studies. Unlike Barth, who remains interested in cultural variation, Cohen delimits the field to political processes involving informal corporate groups. In order to obtain the support of their potential followers, the leaders of these groups use 'primordial' symbols in their political strategy. As Cohen himself admits, the very term ethnicity may be unfortunate here. Cohen's position, opposed to the primordialism he attributes to Barth, can be described as an instrumentalist view, where the sole *raison d'être* of ethnicity and ethnic organisation lies in its political functioning. In this view, ethnicity needs no historical or cultural explanation: it arises entirely from contemporary social conditions (see chapter 5).

A critic of Cohen's position might ask why it is that certain symbols are effective and certain ethnic configurations are possible, while others are not. If ethnic identities are created wholly through political processes, then it should have been possible to create any identity at all. Then it would, for example, have been possible to persuade members of the Maasai ethnic category in Kenya that they were really Kikuyus. Since such a feat is evidently not possible, ethnicity must have a non-instrumental, non-political element. However, to be fair, Cohen's main argument is that it is the formation and functioning of ethnic corporate groups that matter sociologically and should provide the focus for research. In this regard, he is on safe ground in arguing that such groups, far from being 'primordial', are aspects of processes of change – frequently urbanisation and migration. What he does not discuss is the nature of the stuff on which these groups feed. So, it seems, the shared identity of the individuals who eventually form an ethnic group is taken for granted after all in Cohen's model.

Whether Barth is a primordialist or not is a debatable point. The distinction between primordialist and instrumentalist views of ethnicity can be useful chiefly because it highlights a crucial duality in ethnicity (see Shils, 1980; Geertz, 1973 [1963] for primordialist positions). The 'organisational vessels' referred to by Barth must have some kind of purpose in order to operate, and they must simultaneously have some kind of appeal to their target group that justifies group allegiance. This point is elegantly driven home by Cohen in his *Two-dimensional Man* (A. Cohen, 1974b), where the main argument is that ethnic organisation must simultaneously serve political ends *and* satisfy psychological needs for belongingness and meaning.

A second controversy can be described as the relationship between 'subjectivist' and 'objectivist' views on ethnicity. Barth's perspective, where ethnicity is defined as categorical ascriptions undertaken by the agents themselves, is usually regarded as a subjectivist position. An opposing view would hold that ethnic distinctions, ethnic organisation or even ethnic stratification may well exist without the acquiescence or even the awareness of the agents themselves. Typical objectivist perspectives either approach ethnicity as observable characteristics of social organisation, rejecting subjective ascription as an important criterion of ethnicity (Cohen's appoach), or stress large-scale historical processes and power differences inherent in the social structure as determinants of ethnicity, rather than strategic action (cf. chapter 5). To some anthropologists, a focus on self-ascription, social classification and strategic action may represent either an unwanted intrusion of psychology into what is essentially a sociological discipline, or a neglect of large-scale historical processes which may be instrumental in determining ethnic relations at the interpersonal level.

A related controversy concerns the notion of 'situational selection', which seems to presuppose that agents are free to choose their actions and whether to under- or overcommunicate ethnic identity. Can ethnicity simultaneously be an imperative status *and* subject to situational selection and choice, or are the two views mutually exclusive? In a major review article, Jonathan Okamura (1981) notes that the anthropologists who have written about situational ethnicity tend to emphasise either the *cognitive* aspect (choice and strategy) or the *structural* aspect (constraints imposed upon actors) of interethnic situations.

This difference in emphasis, as well as the difference between subjectivist and objectivist views of ethnicity, pertains to a fundamental duality in the social disciplines; the distinction, as Holy and Stuchlik

(1983: 1) succinctly put it, between 'approaches that study how societies, social systems, or structures function, and approaches that study why people do the things they do'. This difference in perspective is sometimes described as the distinction between a Weberian and a Durkheimian view of social life. Anthony Giddens is an important spokesman for the fusion of the two perspectives. In his theory of structuration (Giddens, 1979; 1984), social life is seen as fundamentally dual, comprising both agency and structure simultaneously; both freedom and constraint, if one prefers.

Studies of ethnicity highlight the interrelationship between choice and constraint. A Pathan may under certain circumstances choose to become a Baluch, but this deprives him of rights in Pathan society and gives him new obligations to a Baluch chief. A Mauritian Creole may choose to undercommunicate her ethnic identity situationally, but she cannot eliminate it altogether. In a plural society such as Guyana, Indo-Guyanese, who are largely smallholders, can choose how they would like to allocate their resources and may even climb socially to a white-collar job, but they cannot choose away the ethnic division of labour and the Afro-Guyanese political hegemony. In a friendly critique of Barth's emphasis on individual choice, Sandra Wallman concludes: 'The ultimate constraint must lie in the fact that no one can take up an option which is not there' (Wallman, 1986: 233). In a more polemical vein, Worsley has written:

Many interactionist studies of ethnicity at the level of the community are vitiated by a liberal metaphysic developed in open societies, where a degree of choice exists for the individual to consciously decide whether to assimilate or not, and where social mobility is permitted and significant. The individual is thus taken as the jumping-off point in the analysis, and choice is assumed to be the crucial social fact. Life, it would seem, is a market, or a cafeteria. (Worsley, 1984: 246)

Ethnic identities are neither ascribed nor achieved: they are both. They are wedged between situational selection and imperatives imposed from without. I have up to now emphasised the cognitive and voluntary aspects of ethnicity. From now on we shall oscillate somewhat between the two perspectives, trying to show how, as Marx wrote, people make history, but not under circumstances of their own choosing.

Although these differences in emphasis may be important and may reflect fundamental theoretical differences, it seems appropriate to end this chapter by noting some of the many similarities between the research strategies which have been presented so far (with the possible exception of pluralist theory). Most social anthropologists who study ethnicity agree on certain vital points developed, inter alia, by Barth and his associates, although there is disagreement on where to put the emphasis.

There is general agreement concerning the relativity and relational character of ethnic identity, and it has been well documented that there is no simple relationship between cultural variation and the formation of ethnic groups. There is also widespread agreement that notions of cultural differences and processes of boundary maintenance arise from aspects of social organisation, not from 'objective cultural differences'. The studies discussed in this chapter have focused on the social organisational or political aspect of ethnicity; its potential for organising the interests of groups, often in situations of group competition. In the following chapters I shall indicate how the anthropological study of ethnicity has branched off in various directions, now paying greater attention to the identity side of ethnicity, ideology, the historical creation of ethnicity and the ethnic creation of history, and power relations.

4 ETHNIC IDENTITY AND IDEOLOGY

> [I]f we are to understand ... 'the persisting facts of ethnicity', then I believe that we need to supplement conventional sociological perspectives by paying greater attention to the nature of ethnic identity.
>
> A.L. Epstein (1978: 5)

In the two previous chapters, we have considered aspects of ethnicity from a largely behaviourist point of view. Processes of social inclusion and exclusion, and forms of ethnic incorporation, have been described in relation to interaction and social integration. Such a perspective does allow for an investigation of the symbolic aspect of ethnicity – the ethnic identity – yet this dimension is generally seen as a concomitant, or even an effect, of social process, individual utility or social functionality. This chapter will discuss how ethnic identity may assume fundamental importance for the individual; how attachment and loyalty to ethnic categories or groups are created and maintained. In order to deal with this topic, we need to understand how individuals perceive and classify their social surroundings, and also how the past is used to make sense of the present. Notions of shared origins are usually crucial for ethnic identity, and interpretations of history are therefore important to ideologies seeking to justify, strengthen and maintain particular ethnic identities.

Approaches focusing on the identity aspect of ethnicity were for a long time met with scepticism in social anthropology. Since social anthropology deals with processes taking place *between* people, and since identity has conventionally been held to exist *inside* each individual, the study of personal identity was for a long time neglected by anthropologists. In recent years there have nonetheless been considerable advances in the anthropological study of identity. It has been shown that aspects of the person which have conventionally been held to be unchangeable, inner and private, may fruitfully be studied as symbolic aspects of social processes. In other words, that which was formerly considered private and fixed is now increasingly held to be public and negotiable. In cross-cultural studies of emotions, it has been argued that emotions, far from being innate, are socially created (Rosaldo, 1984; Howell and Willis, 1989). Similarly, studies of ethnicity have demonstrated the relationship between social processes and personal identities (for example Epstein, 1978; 1992).

In anthropological discourse, identity means *being the same as oneself* as well as *being different*. In Jean-Marie Benoist's words, the study of identity must 'oscillate between the poles of disconnected singularity and globalising unity' (Benoist, 1977: 15). When we talk of identity in social anthropology, we refer to social identity, not to the depths of the individual mind. We must therefore begin by looking at social relations and social organisation.

If we want to understand ethnic identity, we cannot a priori assume that ethnic categories exist by virtue of certain 'functions'. This implies that in order to come to grips with ethnic identity, we must try to understand what it is about ethnic classification and categorical belongingness that makes sense to the people involved.

Order in the social universe

Since the publication of Durkheim's and Mauss' *Primitive Classification* (1964 [1903]), the study of classification has been a central concern in anthropology. Claude Lévi-Strauss (1962), Mary Douglas (1966; 1970) and many others have demonstrated that humans are classifying animals who distinguish between kinds or classes of phenomena. Classification is a kind of native theory whereby the infinite complexity of the experienced world is reduced to a finite number of categories.

The kinds of classification developed in any society are necessarily related to that society's organisation and way of life. Thus the Nuer have more than fifteen words for different colour patterns of cattle (Evans-Pritchard, 1940), and some Inuit groups have twenty-five words for different kinds of snow. The classifications of plants and animals are not objective, but rather social constructions. Thus, while Europeans classify the cassowary as a bird, the Karam of New Guinea do not. For them, it cannot be a bird since birds fly and the cassowary does not. However, bats are classified together with birds (Bulmer, 1967).

Ethnic classifications are also social and cultural products related to the requirements of the classifiers. They serve to order the social world and to create standardised cognitive maps over categories of relevant others.

Taking as his point of departure the earlier Copperbelt studies undertaken by himself and his colleagues, Epstein (1978) asks how it could be that the hundreds of ethnic categories present in the larger towns on the Copperbelt could be reduced to a handful of groups in social classification. People who belonged to different 'tribes' were lumped together in general categories. The reason is that ethnic taxonomies tend to become less detailed with increasing perceived social distance from oneself. In Europe it is therefore common to think of 'Africans' or 'North American Indians' as ethnic categories, although each of these 'groups' comprises hundreds of mutually exclusive ethnic categories. Clearly, it would have been unpractical (and in most cases impossible) to make hundreds of fine distinctions between categories of people: usually, one will limit oneself to making those distinctions which are socially relevant (see chapter 2).

Ethnic classification can thus be seen as a practical way of creating order in the social universe. Racial theory, which was a respectable branch of physical anthropology in the Victorian age, endeavoured to divide humanity into four mutually exclusive 'races', and it can retrospectively be seen as a typical attempt to classify the bewildering variety of humans into a few unambiguous categories. In a similar way (but with much less devastating effects), the townspeople of the Copperbelt divided their neighbours into a few standardised categories.

In Britain, the ethnic category 'West Indians' has been applied for decades to immigrants from dozens of different islands and territories: Guyanese, Trinidadians, Jamaicans, Barbadians and 'small-islanders' are considered members of the same ethnic group, although they regard themselves as members of different groups. Eventually, the British ascriptive category 'West Indian' may become an integral part of their own identity: they may start to regard themselves as West Indians, even if such a label was scarcely relevant in their country of origin. Eventually, they may even classify themselves with descendants of Africans as Black British. In extreme cases, even a categorical ascription like 'immigrant' may be applied to people from a dominant group – and it may include people with highly different cultural backgrounds, say, from Chile to Vietnam.

The creation of loyalty to nations follows a similar logic. With the emergence of nationalist ideology and nation-states, people are being taught that they are not primarily from Paris, Savoie, Languedoc or wherever, but that they should instead define themselves as French (Weber, 1976). If such an ideological pressure is successful, the compass of one's community thereby increases many times.

Apart from illustrating the general point that social identities are relational, these examples suggest that there is a close relationship between identities and social circumstances. Identities may change as society changes, and they are certainly not as 'inner', as private and immutable, as common sense may sometimes insist. Systems of social classification and principles of inclusion and exclusion always create order, but the kind of order created is related to aspects of the wider social system.

Anomalies

Every social community or identity is exclusive in the sense that not everybody can take part. Groups and collectivities are always constituted in relation to *others*. A shared European identity, for example, would have to define itself in contrast to Muslim, Middle Eastern or Arab identity, possibly also in relation to African, East Asian and North American identities – depending on the social situation.

The boundaries of ethnic groups, we have seen in chapters 2 and 3, are relative and vary situationally in significance. There are situations where ethnicity is relatively unimportant, and there are situations where it provides a decisive mechanism for exclusion and inclusion as well as clear guidelines for behaviour. However, there are also contexts where it may be difficult to ascribe a definite ethnic identity to an individual. If your father is a Cree Indian and your mother is an Francophone Canadian, or vice versa, what about yourself? What is likely to be the religion of the children of an Indian Muslim and a Hindu? People who are 'betwixt and between', to use Victor Turner's (1967) apt phrase, can be numerous and tend to mess up any neat system of contrasts in ethnic classification. I shall propose, following Mary Douglas (1966), to call them *ethnic anomalies*. They can be considered as 'neither-nor' or 'both-and', depending on the situation and/or the wider context.

A typical 'anomalous' ethnic category is that made up by second- and third-generation immigrants in Europe, or rather, the children and children's children of immigrants. They may consider themselves, and may be considered by others, as members of the same ethnic group as their parents; yet they may also consider themselves as having 'adapted' to the majority culture. They are often bilingual in their mother-tongue and the national language of the host country. Some of them have double citizenship, and many experience conflicting loyalties. In some situations, they are expected to be individualistic and independent-minded; in others, they are expected to be obedient and loyal. Typically, the children of Pakistani immigrants to Norway claim that they do not properly feel at home either in Norway or in Pakistan. Provided that these groups are permanent minorities, there are two likely outcomes of this situation: assimilation to the dominant group or ethnic incorporation. The former option presupposes that the dominant group allows new members (which is not always the case). The latter option has two varieties: the anomalous group may branch off and declare itself an ethnic category; or its members may continue to be loyal to their grandparents' ethnic category, although they are conscious of being culturally different.

An illustration of the first alternative could be the development of 'Black British' as an ethnic category. Black British are neither African nor Caribbean, although their ancestors were either African or Caribbean. They have no other country than Britain and no other vernacular than that classified by linguists as Black British English. They have clubs, informal associations and frequently a sense of solidarity, and may to this effect be considered an ethnic category.

The other alternative consists of insisting that one is still an X, even if one has taken on some of the habits of the Ys. In this way, the considerable population of Indian origin in Britain has managed to develop and maintain Indo-British identities, although there is great cultural variation within the category. Some 'British Indians' seem to have a very British way of life, whereas others seem very traditional (cf. Rushdie, 1991: ch. 1).[1] This does not have to be more difficult than maintaining English identity, which is normally unproblematic despite great cultural variation within the category of people whose members define themselves, and are defined by others, as English (cf. also chapter 7).

For the kind of ethnic anomaly described here, problems arise chiefly in relation to *gatekeeping*. If one is simultaneously a member of two groups which are partly defined through mutual contrasting, difficult situations are inevitable. Drawing on earlier discussions of culture and identity, we may argue that this is not necessarily because the 'cultures' are incompatible, but because the ethnic ideologies hold that they are. In a social environment where one is expected to have a well-defined ethnic identity, it may be psychologically and socially difficult to 'bet on two horses'.

The offspring of 'mixed' couples are a different kind of ethnic anomalies, although their identity problems may be similar to those

---

1 Consider the author V.S. Naipaul's situation for an extreme case. He is an East Indian from the West Indies (Naipaul, 1973), a Trinidadian descendant of indentured labourers from India. Imagine his attempts to explain his ethnic identity to foreigners!

of the children or grandchildren of immigrants. In colonial Haiti, an extremely detailed taxonomic system was developed in order to distinguish between people with varying 'racial' origins. An individual with 127 parts 'white' and one part 'black' was defined as a *sang-mêlé* (of mixed blood). In other societies, people are less scientifically inclined and distinctions tend to be less meticulous.

In some societies, 'mixed' people are very numerous. Sometimes, separate labels are invented for them, such as 'Eurasian' in some South-East Asian societies, or *gen de couleur* in the former French sugar colonies. In some cases, they become distinctive ethnic categories with tendencies towards ethnic incorporation. In Mauritius, the Mulattoes or *gens de couleur* have traditionally occupied a distinct place in the division of labour (white-collar and middle-managerial jobs); they have their own clubs and informal associations, and may be considered an ethnic category. Some of them even argue that they are the only true Mauritians, since they are the only group that grew out of Mauritian soil – the only non-immigrants. Stable 'mixed' ethnic categories have also developed elsewhere. In certain societies in South and Central America, for example, people considered as 'racially mixed', notably Mestizos, have gradually become permanent ethnic categories with more or less clear boundaries, external symbols communicating their cultural distinctiveness, and rules of endogamy. In other societies, such as urban Brazil, skin colour represents a continuum with no clear boundaries or corporate groupings; it does not express ethnicity.

Ethnic anomalies are often lumped with one of the groups, usually the lowest-ranking one. This has happened to North American 'Mulattoes', who are defined as blacks. Others may find themselves in uncomfortable 'betwixt-and-between' situations, such as the Trinidadian *douglas*. *Dougla* is a Bhojpuri word meaning 'bastard', and the *douglas* are Trinidadians with one Indian and one African parent. It almost goes without saying that their identity problem can be severe in a society where the main classificatory principle contrasts Africans and Indians.

In modern state societies, it may be socially necessary to develop unambiguous delineations of ethnic identity. Particularly in situations where certain ethnic groups are granted special rights, 'objective' definitions of ethnicity have been created. In Norway, one has the right to consider oneself Sami if at least one grandparent used Sami as his or her first language. According to Jewish ideology, anybody with a Jewish mother has the right to consider him- or herself a Jew. In Canadian legislation, Roosens (1989) explains, the criteria for Indian identity have changed at several points in recent history. With the recent introduction of special rights for Indians and the rise of powerful Indian interest groups, it has become important to decide on clear criteria for inclusion and exclusion. Whereas the Norwegian state decided on a linguistic criterion for Sami-ness, the Canadian state decided, in a law passed in 1951, on a pseudo-biological criterion. If one's father was an Indian, one had the right to be considered an Indian. In terms of genetics, this is an arbitrary distinction; in terms of culture, it is probably even more so, and the example is interesting in indicating how biology and 'race' are culturally constructed. In other words, although contrasting ethnic classifications and bounded identities may seem tidy on paper (and in native theory, including national statistics!), they are more complicated and knotty in actual societies.

Entrepreneurs

Do people, when all is said and done, create their identities, or do they inadvertently express aspects of their society through their social selves? To put it differently: should anthropology stress the voluntary, chosen and strategic aspects of agency and social identity, or should it rather concentrate on showing the ways in which humans are products of culture and society? There is no definite answer to these questions, but the choice of perspective can make for important differences in the resulting analyses. In describing *douglas*, second-generation immigrants and Indian 'half-castes' as anomalies, I have essentially viewed them as creations of society. They become anomalies by virtue of pre-existing classificatory categories which they can do little to change. In this way, the Barthian view of ethnicity as a system of mutually exclusive self-ascriptions must be slightly modified: the ascriptions undertaken by *others* may also contribute to creating ethnicity. People may be *forced* to take on an ethnic identity, even if they would have preferred not to (cf. Lock, 1990).

An actor-centred perspective on 'anomalous' ethnic categories might lead to a different conclusion. For just as it can be shown that individuals who fall between acknowledged categories are defined 'by the system' as anomalous, sometimes morally suspect outsiders, they may also exploit this ambiguity to their own advantage. Instead of seeing these individuals as anomalies, one may regard them as entrepreneurs or cultural brokers who turn the classificatory ambiguities to their own advantage (Paine, 1971). A Mauritian friend, who is of partly Tamil, partly mixed (*gen de couleur*) origin and whose name is, appropriately, Christian Saminaden, sometimes exploits this ambiguity in such a way. When dealing with Tamils or Hindus he stresses his

Saminaden aspect, but if he does business with Catholics he is primarily Christian.

Whether one regards this kind of fuzzy ethnic category as anomalous or as an entrepreneurial category is partly a matter of theoretical perspective, but it also depends on the empirical context. In some societies, for some individuals and in some situations, it may be more or less difficult or profitable to be a 'between and betwixt' person. And we should not a priori assume that having an ambiguous ethnic identity implies having no roots and no culture and is therefore unbearable. An assumption to this effect is perhaps neither more nor less than an expression of English native theory; and before assuming that ethnic anomalies are by default unhappy, we ought to look into their actual lives.

There is no doubt that societies differ strongly on this score. In some societies, identities are to a greater extent chosen than in others. Ernest Gellner (1991) has in this context introduced what he calls 'the potato principle', referring to the strongly territorial identity and feeling of 'rootedness' which he assumes to be prevalent among peasants. In such societies there is little social mobility, and people are tied to a place and to webs of kinship and patron–client relationships. Gellner contrasts this kind of identity with the more fluid identities typical of industrial societies where social mobility is considerable and individual choice is a major value. The contrast may be oversimplifying. We should nevertheless keep in mind that ethnic identities are flexible to a highly varying degree.

Analogic and digital; we and us

Ethnic categorisations can be analysed as attempts to create order in, and make sense of, a bewildering chaos of different 'kinds' of people. And, as we have just seen, this kind of map creates its own problems because the territory it describes is more complex than itself. Both natives and anthropologists therefore run into paradoxes and contradictions when they try to apply a stylised ethnic taxonomy consistently.

In the discussions of ethnicity in the Copperbelt and Mauritius in chapter 2, I pointed out that people classify others not only along the axis of identity versus difference (the basic Us–Them mechanism), but also according to perceived *degrees* of difference. For a Kamba in Kenya, the Kikuyu and other Bantu-speaking peoples are perceived as closer than Luo and other groups who speak Nilotic languages. To a Swede, a Dane is considered closer than a German, who is in turn considered closer than a Hungarian. Bogardus-type scales of perceived social distance can here be helpful in mapping out such differences, although we should keep in mind that actual behaviour does not necessarily correspond to expectations which may arise from interviews.

In a complex multi-ethnic environment, agents will thus develop different standardised forms of behaviour vis-à-vis different categories of others. Some are perceived as 'almost like ourselves'; others are perceived as 'extremely different from us'. When such principles of exclusion and inclusion allow for differences of degree, we may call them *analogic*. They do not encourage the formation of unambiguous, clear-cut boundaries. When, on the contrary, systems of classification operate on an unambiguous inclusion/exclusion basis where all outsiders are regarded as 'more or less the same', they may be spoken of as *digital*.

Further, the communities whose existence is postulated by ethnic ideologies may be seen as expressions of different aspects of community. Here we can distinguish between two modalities of group solidarity, which we may, following Sartre (1943), call *we-hood* and *us-hood*, respectively.[2] Being *us*, people are loyal and socially integrated chiefly in relation to *the other*; through competition, enmity, symbiosis or the contrastive use of stereotypes and boundary symbols. Being *we*, on the other hand, entails being integrated because of shared activities within the collectivity.

Although ethnicity, being relational, is by definition a phenomenon of us-hood, the ethnic category or group must additionally have an element of we-hood in order to be viable – a shared language or religion, a division of labour which creates interdependence, or a notion of shared origins. I shall now turn to an exploration of the ways in which ethnic ideologies use notions of shared culture to define and delimit ethnic identity.

The emergence of ethnic identities

Epstein (1978) notes that many of the societies traditionally studied by anthropologists are undergoing rapid processes of social and cultural change, yet ethnicity – contrary to many expectations – does not vanish as a result, but instead emerges in a new, often more powerful and more clearly articulated form. Epstein states:

[S]ince ethnicity arises so often in circumstances of social upheaval and transformation, which are frequently accompanied by severe cultural erosion and

---

2 French has no word for 'us', and Sartre therefore distinguishes between 'we-as-subject' and 'we-as-object'.

the disappearance of many customs that might serve as marks of distinctiveness, a critical issue is *how that identity is to be maintained* over a number of generations. (Epstein, 1978: xiii, my emphasis)

Ethnic symbolism referring to the ancient language, religion, kinship system or way of life is crucial for the maintenance of ethnic identity through periods of change. Generally speaking, social identity becomes most important the moment it seems threatened. Several factors may constitute such a perceived threat, but they are always related to some kind of change – migration, change in the demographic situation, industrialisation or other economic change, or integration into or encapsulation by a larger political system (cf. chapter 5).

Conspicuous forms of boundary maintenance become important when the boundaries are under pressure. Ethnic identities, which embody a perceived continuity with the past, may in this way function in a psychologically reassuring way for the individual in times of upheaval; they seem to tell people that although 'all that is solid melts into air' (Marx; cf. Berman, 1982), there is an unchanging, stable core of ethnic belongingness which assures the individual of a continuity with the past, which can be an important source of self-respect and personal authenticity in the modern world, which is often perceived as a world of flux and make-believe. If one can claim to 'have a culture', it proves that one is faithful to one's ancestors and to the past. Religion may or may not play an important part here. Many ethnic movements are religious in character and stress the importance of religious conformity to their members, but other movements may be just as efficient, with respect to both politics and identity, without such a component.

Ethnic identities can be seen as expressions of metaphoric kinship. Some notion of shared descent may be a universal element in ethnic ideologies (Nash, 1988; Yelvington, 1991). Notions of 'race' are sometimes, but not always, part of such ideologies. Sometimes ethnic ideologies, like kin genealogies, trace common descent back to a known ancestor, although the actual linkages are unknown.

The formation of new ethnic categories, which presupposes the formation of new identities, generally follows one of two possible paths. First, it may come about through an extension of existing identifications; it may thus be argued that all Aymara (a category of Andes Indians) are descendants of a particular pre-Columbian people, and that all Aymaras should therefore be loyal to the Aymara group as a whole and not just to their extended lineage or village. Similarly, in the creation of a Norwegian ethnic identity in the nineteenth century, an imputed genealogical continuity with early medieval Viking chiefs was stressed as an argument for the uniqueness of Norwegians in relation to Swedes and Danes, who were culturally close.

The second possibility is the reverse: it consists in reducing the size of the group with presumed shared ancestry. A common sociological term for this kind of process is 'fission'. At the levels of ideology and personal identity, it can be expressed through a shallowing of genealogies. Instead of tracing one's group origins back to, say, Adam or Noah, one may thus trace it back to one of their respective sons (or to a more recent ancestor – compare the 'twelve tribes of Israel') and thereby argue the validity of present ethnic boundaries.

Both of these possibilities for the delineation of ethnic identities require reinterpretations of the past. The notion of ancestry is itself ambiguous. For if a shared ethnic identity presupposes a notion of shared ancestry, how many generations should one feel compelled to go back in order to find a starting point for one's present ethnic identity? There is no objective answer to that question: the answer is conditional on the social context.

This aspect of ethnic identity also indicates that there is no simple one-to-one relationship between ideology and social practices. For although Jews justify their ethnic identity by referring to shared ancestry, it is evident that all Jews do not have the same ancestry. Jews from Eastern Europe tend to look like East Europeans, and Jews from North Africa tend to look like North Africans. Despite an ideology of endogamy, there has been considerable de facto interbreeding with the surrounding populations.

Finally, the criterion of imputed shared origins seriously reduces the possible number of ethnic categories in any society. It is true that ethnicity is a social creation and not a fact of nature, and ethnic variation does not correspond to cultural variation. But ethnic identities must seem convincing to their members in order to function – and they must also be acknowledged as legitimate by non-members of the group. If a group of London punks insist that they have a unique culture with origins in a mythical and misty past, their potential for becoming an ethnic category depends on the recognition of others. Similarly, if someone claims that Indians and Africans have the same origins and should therefore be considered an ethnic group, he or she will probably not be successful, since most Africans and Indians would disagree.

In recent years, anthropologists have been concerned with the ways in which history and cultural symbols are manipulated in the creation of ethnic identities and organisations. Such a focus implies that ethnic identity is in an important sense *constructed*, and we will now consider a few examples indicating how this happens.

The creation of an ancestral identity

The Huron Indians of Québec are today a respected Canadian 'tribe' (Roosens, 1989). Unlike many other indigenous peoples, they have succeeded in presenting themselves to society at large as an oppressed people with a unique, if vanishing, culture, who have for centuries been harassed, massacred and deprived of civil and territorial rights by the colonialists and the Canadian authorities. A comparison between the ethnic leaders' presentation of their case and the facts presented in historical records shows that it is possible to go very far in the reinterpretation of history in order to create collective identity and political cohesion.

Historical monographs dealing with the Hurons indicate that their contacts with the colonisers were for centuries both voluntary and profitable. They were sedentary and acted as intermediaries between French fur traders and the nomadic hunters who provided the furs in the sixteenth and early seventeenth centuries. Later, they were in regular contact with Jesuit missionaries, who were nevertheless unsuccessful in their attempts to convert them.

The Hurons' main enemies were the Iroquois. In the mid-seventeenth century the Iroquois began to attack Huron villages with unprecedented intensity, and the survivors were dispersed. Most of them were assimilated into Iroquois groups, and some fled to Québec. It was during this period that traditional Huron culture, as well as their language, vanished. Later, they collaborated with the French and were for this reason granted a hunting area to which they had no aboriginal claim.

An influential Huron version of their history differs from this version on a number of points. It is presented in a book by their Chief Max Gros-Louis, *Le premier des Hurons* (1981; reference in Roosens, 1989). The book does not acknowledge that there were traditional enmities between Indian tribes in general and between the Hurons and the Iroquois in particular. It is also suggested that such enmities, if they occurred, were incited by the colonialists. According to Roosens, the book also depicts 'a kind of pan-Indian culture', which 'unites all Indians against all outsiders and primarily against the whites'. This 'culture', as described and reified in Gros-Louis' book, is composed of elements which conform to widespread positive stereotypes of Indians in Euro-Canadian society. The Indians are depicted as being close to nature and full of respect for plants and animals; they are spontaneously hospitable, extremely honest, incorruptible and have great personal integrity; they are tolerant and mild-mannered, and are open-minded in respect to foreign cultures.

In brief, 'Indian culture' is depicted as superior to the 'white' one in a number of regards.

Roosens' rather uncharitable conclusion is that this 'Indian culture' is an invention which may be politically efficient but which is one-sided, 'to put it mildly'. That the Hurons have achieved their present position is, he argues, through the deliberate creation of an *ethnic counterculture*, including a rendering of their history and presentation of their ancestral culture which may be described as very inventive. Roosens concludes:

When I compared the characteristics of this neo-Huron culture with the culture depicted in the historical records, most of the modern traits, virtually everything, were 'counterfeit': the folklore articles, the hair style, the mocassins, the 'Indian' parade costumes, the canoes, the pottery, the language, the music. (Roosens, 1989: 47)

History and ideology

Selective renderings of history are not confined to ethnic minorities such as the Hurons. Historians working in modern European nation-states have taken great pains to demonstrate that their nations are really very old, although they were usually created in the nineteenth century (Anderson, 1991 [1983]). This may be a feature of modernity. In his book about the Hurons, Chief Gros-Louis effectively turned 'Indian culture' into *an object*, regarding it from the outside, as something existing independently of whatever activities the actual Hurons might be involved in. When culture is reified in this way, it can be manipulated. Thus, several Hurons have in recent years taken Indian names and have begun to wear Indian clothing, as self-conscious ways of communicating that they 'have a culture'. This kind of personal identity politics is characteristic of modern societies.

Imputed aboriginality and continuity with the past can be important sources of political legitimacy. Simultaneously, knowledge of one's own history (whether fabricated or not) can be highly important in the fashioning of ethnic identity. Genealogies, both personal and cultural ones, are always written in selective ways – both for political and other reasons. Thus many white North Americans who have traced their origins have found English nobility among their ancestors. The fact that their family trees probably contain prostitutes and manual workers as well is undercommunicated. Similarly, Huron Indians and other Indian groups in North America would undercommunicate the fact that many of their ancestors were in fact Europeans; that mixed marriages have been common for a very long time.

At this juncture, many anthropologists would part company with professional historians in the study of ethnogenesis. While many historians tend to try to find out what *really* happened – some even distinguish between 'invented' traditions and 'real' traditions (Hobsbawm, 1983; cf. chapter 5) – most anthropologists would rather concentrate on showing the ways in which particular historical accounts are used as tools in the *contemporary* creation of identities and in politics. Anthropologists would stress that history is not a product of the past but a response to requirements of the present. For that reason, this discussion of history relates not to the past but to the present. In the next chapter, I shall look into the past itself.

An example of a reconstructed history which has been only partly successful concerns the Muslims in Mauritius (Eriksen, 1988; 1990). Comprising about 17 per cent of the Mauritian population, all Mauritian Muslims are descendants of merchants and indentured labourers who came from British India in the eighteenth and nineteenth centuries. Their languages were Bhojpuri, Sindhi and Gujerati; a few were literate in Urdu. At the 1972 population census, virtually all of the Muslims stated that their ancestral language was an Indian language. (Urdu, being a prestige language, was overrepresented.) By the next census ten years later, however, more than half of the Muslims stated that their ancestral language was Arabic. During the 1970s a powerful pan-Arabic movement had emerged, and with the oil crisis in 1974 it became evident that the Arabs represented a considerable force in world politics. It became more interesting to be a part of this movement than to direct one's roots towards Pakistan or India. Thus the Mauritian Muslims redefined their ancestral culture. In the capital, Port-Louis, Muslim women began to wear veils and the men started to wear long white robes and grow beards. They tried, effectively, to become descendants of Arabs instead of being descendants of Indian labourers. However, this turn towards the Arab world was generally not acknowledged by other Mauritians, and many pointed out that, really, the Muslims were just as Indian as the Hindus. The new identity was, in other words, a contested one. During the 1980s the orientation towards the Arab world was lessened somewhat, but it should be noted that many Mauritian Muslims supported Iraq during the Gulf war, although both Mauritius and Pakistan were on the Allied side.

These two examples, the Hurons and the Mauritian Muslims, may appear almost as parodies of ethnic groups, but they are more typical than they may seem. Interpretations of the past are important to every ethnic identity, and the relationship between such interpretations and 'objective history' is necessarily contestable. As Lévi-Strauss has argued in a comparison between myth and history (Lévi-Strauss, 1962), historical accounts include only a minute fraction of all the events that have taken place in a certain timespan, and they necessarily involve interpretation and selection.

Since it is not 'objective culture' that shapes ethnicity, it makes sense to state that ethnic identities can be maintained despite cultural change. However, such an identity maintenance may seem para-doxical, since ethnic ideologies stress the continuity of that very cultural content as a justification for the continued existence and cohesion of the group. An important point in Leach's (1954) study of Kachin politics is that there is never a perfect fit between ideology and social practices. Leach shows that the same Kachin myths and cosmology can be used to justify two highly different ideal social orders, *gumlao* and *gumsa*, which are egalitarian and hierarchical, respectively (Leach, 1954: ch. 3). This ambiguity or 'multivocality' of symbols (V. Turner, 1967) makes it possible to manipulate them polit-ically. Thus, in Sri Lanka Tamils and Sinhalese have slightly different versions of the same myths: both of them have created versions tailored to fit their respective political projects (Kapferer, 1988). Just as individuals can romanticise their childhoods, it seems, ethnic groups can acquire a tragic and heroic history. And, as the Comaroffs state, 'while ethnicity is the product of specific historical processes, it tends to take on the "natural" appearance of an autonomous force, a "principle" capable of determining the course of social life' (Comaroff and Comaroff, 1992: 60). What we are looking at here is thus not the past, but present-day *constructions* of the past.

Social factors in identity processes

Culture is in a sense invented, and the relationship between culture as ideology and culture as fact is tenuous. Yet it is evident that anything will not function equally well in the social legitimation of ethnic identities. If the agents themselves hold that a certain descrip-tion of their culture is obviously false, it cannot provide them with a powerful ethnic identity. If a group's version of its cultural history is seriously contested by other groups, as was the case with the Mauritian Muslims, it may also be problematic to maintain the identity postulated by that account of history. So we cannot conclude that anything goes and that everything about ethnic identity is deception and make-believe. A principal point throughout this chapter has rather been that identities are ambiguous, and that this ambiguity is connected with a negotiable history and a negotiable cultural content.

Several authors have regarded *utility* as the master variable in accounting for the maintenance of ethnic identity, regarding identity as contingent on ethnic political organisation which is formed in situations of competition over scarce resources. However, notions of utility are themselves cultural creations, and so the boundary between that which is useful and that which is meaningful becomes blurred. It is therefore difficult to predict which ethnic or other identities will be dominant for any given population in the future.

In addition, it has been shown that a number of ethnic categories reproduce their identity even if it actually reduces their chances of attaining prosperity and political power. I have myself written of Mauritian Creole identity along these lines (Eriksen, 1986; 1988): the features of Creole identity which are used internally and externally as identity markers emphasise values which are incompatible with social mobility and political organisation. Individual freedom is seen as a typical Creole 'cultural trait', and it is expressed in ways which make formal political organisation and long-term planning extremely difficult.

It has been argued, along similar lines, that the maintenance of Gypsy identity in Europe should be seen as a cultural and symbolic phenomenon rather than as a competitive strategy. Gypsy society displays different values from mainstream society, and the goals pursued by Gypsies are different from those of the sedentary population (Stewart, 1991; Okely, 1983). For this reason, there is no real competition between the groups. Gypsy identity is thus better viewed as a cultural fact than as an aspect of group competition.

Does European identity exist?

In order to arrive at a better understanding (if not necessarily an explanation) of the development of identities, it may be instructive to look at the historical junctures where new overarching identities are presented, and the processes which lead to their acceptance or rejection. The current attempts to create tighter political and economic integration in the European Community, and the widespread counterreactions to such attempts, may provide interesting material in this regard, and may also suggest what is at stake in attempted redefinitions of identity.

The EC may be regarded as a coordinating organ, an economic market-place and an alliance between independent states. That was how it began in 1957. However, during the late 1980s and the early 1990s it has become a policy of the Community to strengthen integration in important respects. Notably, the transfer of political power from the national capitals to Brussels that is under way implies attempts at redefining loyalties and attachments. A possible consequence of this shift could be that political parties in the European Parliament eventually align themselves along political, not national, lines, so that, say, Greens and Social Democrats will form blocs with Greens and Social Democrats from other European countries instead of aligning themselves with other parties from their own countries. The economic effects of European integration may also be formidable in that, say, French peasants increasingly produce *for Europe* and not for France or their own region. Standardisation of legislation is also progressively taking place.[3]

Will economic and political developments towards European integration lead to the development of a shared European identity? This question has at least three interesting aspects. First, it seems that enthusiasm for European integration is greatest in the poorest regions and among the political and economic elites, which may for different reasons reap the greatest economic and political benefits. In other words, in this regard it seems that identity formation is conditional on perceptions of utility.

Second, economic and political processes are not in themselves sufficient for the development of identity, although they serve as an incentive. Ideology production – notably, the creation of a shared history – is also crucial. Several recent European history books have thus attempted to redraw the past. The most famous is probably Jean-Baptiste Duroselle's *Europe – A History of its Peoples* (Duroselle, 1990), where the author concludes 'it should be possible ... to build a united Europe' (Duroselle, 1990, 414). The book was published simultaneously in several of the European languages. Whereas many earlier history books have stressed the emergence of nation-states and have written history largely from the perspective of the nation, this book explicitly intends to play down the role of individual nations, instead emphasising the shared European heritage as well as the local and regional communities. The outcome is, bluntly phrased, a history of Europe where Greece ostensibly has the same history as Ireland, but not the same history as Turkey[4]. This illustrates the

---

3 Approximately half of the Danish and French populations said 'no' to the Union Treaty of Maastricht, in referendums held in June and September 1992, respectively.

4 Neumann and Welsh (1991) have suggested how 'the Turk' has for centuries served as the significant Other for European identity, in other words how ideas of European identity have depended on contrasting and negative stereotypes of non-Europeans, particularly Turks. Perhaps this factor in European identity may contribute to explaining why Turkey is unlikely to be admitted as an EC/EU member in the near future.

general point that history is open to a variety of interpretations, which may be contested. There are political and economic reasons why nobody endeavours to create a Levantine identity encompassing all the peoples in the eastern Mediterranean, although such an identity might have as much to recommend it in terms of 'objective history' as a European one.

Third, a European identity is not necessarily incompatible with national or ethnic identities (cf. A.D. Smith, 1992). Social identities are segmentary in character, following the general formula described in Evans-Pritchard's (1940) study of Nuer political organisation. Being a member of a family does not preclude being a member of an ethnic group; and being a member of an ethnic group does not necessarily preclude being a member of a more encompassing category. However, for that more encompassing group to exist, it must be *socially relevant*. It must have some goods to deliver – material, political or symbolic – and those goods must be perceived as valuable by the target group.

The question of whether European identity exists or will be viable in the near future cannot be answered straightforwardly. All we can say is that it would have to be conditional on *both* symbolic justification and political organisation.[5]

What do identities do?

Ethnic identity becomes crucially important the moment it is perceived as threatened. Since ethnicity is an aspect of relationship, the importance of boundaries may thus be said to be conditional on the pressure exerted on them. On the other hand, we have seen that expressions of ethnic identity may also be regarded, rather than as psychological responses to threats from the outside or attempts to create order in the social universe, as symbolic tools in political struggles. The social importance of ethnic identities is greatest when the two conditions are fulfilled simultaneously in enacted ethnic ideologies. We shall return to this important point in later chapters.

Identity processes are fundamentally dual and comprise aspects of meaning as well as politics in a wide sense. Functionalist or actor-centred accounts of ethnicity may provide good analyses of ethnic incorporation at the level of interaction and group competition, but

5 Salman Rushdie, incidentally, has identified a kind of proposed identity which, apparently, does not work; namely, that linked with the Commonwealth. Being interviewed as a 'Commonwealth writer', he had to admit that he found 'this strange term, "Commonwealth literature", unhelpful and even a little distasteful' (Rushdie, 1991: 61).

they usually decline to ask why it is that ethnic identities are so pervasive and fundamental to people; why, as Benedict Anderson (1991 [1983]) puts it, people are willing to die for their nation (or ethnic community) but usually not for their social class or city. I have deliberately not given a simple answer to this very complex question here, but have instead shown a variety of ways in which it can meaningfully be asked without recourse to pure speculation.

The next chapter will approach the questions of ethnic identity and group formation from a perspective which is complementary to those emphasised so far. We now turn to assessing the importance of historical and societal macro processes for the development of ethnic groups and identities. Eventually, it will also be indicated how social anthropology, despite (or perhaps because of) its bias in favour of small-scale societies and interpersonal relations, can be instrumental in creating an understanding of global processes in the contemporary world.

5   ETHNICITY IN HISTORY

[W]hile totemism emerges with the establishment of symmetrical relations between structurally similar social groupings – groupings which may or may not come to be integrated into one political community – ethnicity has its origins in the asymmetrical incorporation of structurally dissimilar groupings into a single political economy.

John and Jean Comaroff (1992: 54)

Where are your parents from? And your grandparents? Your great-grand-parents? Eventually, if the questioner persists, he will find a transplanted root. The 100 per cent American is, after all, 100 per cent something else.

Motto for the Bicentennial Exhibition (1976) at the Smithsonian Institute, Washington, D.C.

The argument and material presented so far seem to suggest that although ethnicity is not confined to modern societies, there are aspects of many interethnic processes which are less likely to come about in non-modern than in modern contexts. In particular, this could be true of reflexive self-identity and that reification of culture which seems to presuppose widespread literacy. The contemporary phenomena of nationalism and minority issues are clearly confined to the modern world. It could be argued that pre-colonial notions of cultural differences refer to different kinds of phenomena altogether from those engendered by capitalism and the state (Southall, 1970; Fardon, 1987). On the other hand, we should be aware that the various ethnic processes analysed in Barth (1969b) largely take place in non-modern settings.

This chapter will analyse the process of 'ethnogenesis' – the creation of ethnic relations and ethnic identities – from the perspective of historical change. Several of the theoretical problems discussed in previous chapters will be illuminated here, notably the relationships between ethnicity and modernity, culture and ethnicity, and agency and structure.

The historical development of ethnic relations

In his previously cited essay, Barth (1969a) criticised a then common view on ethnicity for assuming that ethnic phenomena come about due to contact between groups which are already culturally distinctive, often in a colonial setting. Rather, Barth reasons, we should 'ask ourselves what is needed to make ethnic distinctions *emerge* in an area' (Barth, 1969a: 17). What he seems to call for here is an historical perspective on ethnicity. However, neither the book edited by Barth nor most other anthropological studies of ethnicity really undertake the task of showing how ethnic distinctions emerge in an area; how initially homogeneous groups are historically split into two or several distinctive ethnic groups. Barth argues, largely on logical grounds, that occupational specialisation, and the development of some form of group complementarity, will gradually encourage the creation and enactment of distinguishing signs and, eventually, the emergence of distinctive groups, with separate genealogies, each of which considers the others to be culturally distinctive from themselves.

Cultural discontinuity is likely to have developed roughly in this way in a number of settings. In situations where groups simply split and no complementarity develops, cultural variation without ethnicity (defined as the systematic communication of cultural difference) will eventually develop. There are nevertheless great difficulties involved in studying this process empirically, since very long and largely unknown timespans are normally involved. The development of ethnically based political organisation as well as mass movements based on ethnic identity are nevertheless recent (and related to modernisation processes), and that may be a reason why anthropologists have focused on these aspects of 'ethnogenesis'. The political context for the emergence of such ethnic movements has in nearly all cases been a colonial situation or a nation-state.

Expansions of system boundaries

Ethnicity must by definition arise either from a process of social differentiation within a population, which eventually leads to the division of that population into two distinctive groups, or by an expansion of system boundaries bringing hitherto discrete groups into contact with each other. Eric Wolf (1982) has argued that interconnections between societies have been far more widespread than has commonly been assumed by anthropologists, and he demonstrates the importance of such, ultimately global, interconnections from around AD 1400. These connections, Wolf emphasises, cannot all be subsumed under the labels of 'colonialism' or 'the emergence of the capitalist world-system'. In fact, there were important and often wide-reaching regional links of trade, warfare and migration connecting 'tribes' and bands in most parts of the world. Such links also often involved societies which anthropologists have tended to regard as 'cold', after Lévi-Strauss (1962) – unchanging, static societies, in contrast to the 'hot' modern societies which, it is presumed, change perpetually.[1] Wolf's point is that it is misleading to regard the world as an 'archipelago of cultures'; that seemingly discrete societies have always been partly maintained by virtue of their mutual contacts. However, Wolf shows, the intensity and range of these contacts increased greatly with the 'great discoveries' and European colonialism from the fifteenth century onwards. Many ethnic categorisations and ethnic hierarchies still functioning today were the intended or unintended results of European colonialism in North and South America, the Caribbean, Africa, South Asia, East Asia, Australia and the Pacific.

For the sake of clarity, I shall distinguish between four aspects of these processes of change, which have proceeded with uneven pace and in different ways in different societies up to the present. First, we shall look at the consequences of slavery and capitalism for the development of ethnic relations in the New World. Second, the importance of labour migration will be discussed. Third, the importance of naming and semantics – the relationship between language and the non-linguistic world – for the formation of ethnic identities in Africa will be discussed. Fourth, I shall deal with the consequences of social change for identity formation and group organisation. The empirical examples in this chapter are chosen with a view to depicting some of the variation as well as some of the similarities in different kinds of colonial and post-colonial ethnic relationships.

Capitalism

If by ethnicity we refer to the social organisation of communicated cultural differences, ethnicity appeared together with capitalism in many parts of the world. As Epstein (1978; 1992) has shown, 'tribal' relationships in the Copperbelt area were qualitatively different

---

1 This interpretation of Lévi-Strauss is common in the anthropological literature, but it is probably misleading. When he talks of 'cold societies', Lévi-Strauss seems to refer to societies *whose inhabitants* regard them as being essentially static and unchanging. As a matter of fact, these societies certainly do change, although we know little of their history.

before and after colonial pacification, monetarisation and the introduction of labour migrancy and wage work. Before their exodus the
migrants were integrated largely on the village level – politically
through the kin group and economically through subsistence farming
on the ancestral land. They then became political subjects under the
British and participants in a uniform capitalist economic system
based on the individual labour contract and monetary exchange. The
boundaries of the relevant systems expanded enormously. The
migrants entered into horizontal competitive relationships with each
other, and were ranked in an occupational hierarchy with an important
ethnic element: the managerial positions were held by expatriate
Europeans. Where the relevant boundary of the social system formerly
had in many respects been the boundary of the village, it now became
a non-physical boundary, based on the classification of others rather
than their place of residence, their kinship system or their customs.
Interaction across linguistic boundaries increased many times (often
turning languages such as Bemba or English into *linguas francas*),
and as a consequence people became more self-conscious concerning
their origins and cultural identity: they acquired an ethnic identity
with an everyday relevance. Further, as I have argued in chapters 2
and 3, the urban setting offered new opportunities for informal and
formal organisation. The beer-halls, unions and later the political
parties created new possibilities for group organisation. Thus in some
parts of the Copperbelt the 'tribes' emerged as interest groups
organised on the basis of ethnic identity. This form of ethnic organisation was, of course, unknown in pre-colonial times. In this setting,
it was intrinsically linked to capitalism. Furthermore, in such a
situation it became imperative to establish clear criteria for group
membership.

A similar development took place with Canadian Indians, because
of their increased integration into the nation-state. From the moment
Indian identity became a possible vehicle for the acquisition of
particular rights, Indian identity became relevant as an abstract
'umbrella' identity; at the same time, it became important to find clear
criteria for distinguishing between Indians and non-Indians (cf.
chapter 7).

In plantation societies, the introduction of ethnic or 'racial' elements
in the division of labour was perhaps even more apparent. In some
such societies, such as Malaysia and Guyana, different categories of
labourers were systematically recruited from distinctive 'races' or
'groups'. After the abolition of slavery (1835–9), thousands of East
Indians were recruited to many of these societies as indentured
labourers, to replace the former slaves on the sugar plantations. In

these societies, divisions of labour based on colonial ethnic categorisations emerged.

In Mauritius, Indians were recruited as labourers on the canefields,
and the Brahmins among them were hired as *sirdars*, foremen. Many
Creoles (the descendants of slaves) now worked as skilled workers
and artisans at the sugar factories. The middle managerial positions
were held by Chinese and 'Mulattoes', whereas the estate managers
were always Franco-Mauritian (white). In Trinidad, Guyana and Fiji,
the pattern was different; in Trinidad, the foremen were blacks. The
idea that particular categories of people were particularly well
equipped to carry out particular kinds of work gradually became part
and parcel of colonial ideology and practice. Members of different
ascribed groups had different political rights; individuals were ranked
in the economic and political systems according to which category
they were placed in.

Ethnicity, which is today a major social preoccupation and a chief
principle for political organisation in many of these societies (cf.
Nash, 1988, for Malaysia; B. Williams, 1991, for Guyana; Klass, 1991
and Vertovec, 1992, for Trinidad; Eriksen, 1992a, for Mauritius and
Trinidad), must therefore be understood in relation to the colonial
division of labour.

'Black' ethnogenesis

Scientific racism arose in the late eighteenth century, largely as a
response to calls for the abolition of slavery (Todorov, 1989; Banton,
1987). Although most scientists had abandoned the concept of race
by the 1920s, cultural notions of race continue to exist in folk
taxonomies. Personality traits and cultural distinctiveness are in
many societies still attributed to people on the basis of 'race', and it
is in this way that 'races' may become ethnic categories. The physical
appearance of a person may in this sort of society serve as a convenient
shorthand way of telling other members of the society what 'kind of
person' he or she is. Such categorisations, and their accompanying
evaluations and stereotypes, are the work of colonial history and a
particular division of labour and political power; they are no more
natural than the ethnic distinctions differentiating Finns from Swedes.

The African slaves who were transported to the New World and
to the plantation islands in the Indian Ocean from the early sixteenth
century onwards belonged to many different groups who spoke
mutually unintelligible and often unrelated languages, had different
kinship systems and so on. Under different economic and political
circumstances they might well have reproduced their distinctive-

ness after migrating, or they might have merged into other new groups than those they actually did form. As it happened, strict measures were introduced in order to prevent the slaves from retaining a sense of group identity. Families were split up and persons who spoke different languages were compelled to live and work together. As a result, strict legislation dividing people into occupational categories and kinds of political subjects on the basis of colour emerged. Distinctive ethnic categories based on colour became more salient than place of origin or ancestral language. As slaves, and later as an underpaid working class, they were collectively stigmatised by the rulers. By virtue of their identical treatment, they also had shared political interests. In the Caribbean, the United States and the Indian Ocean, a distinctive 'black' ethnic category thus developed, and it is sometimes politically incorporated.

Under different economic and political circumstances, such an ethnic identity would not have been viable: it is far from evident that people of Wolof, Ibo and Ashanti origin should consider themselves members of the same group.

'Black' ethnic identity is relative to social context. In the Caribbean, distinctions are conventionally drawn – and are socially relevant – between blacks and browns. Historically, browns have been a relatively privileged group. Originating as the illicit offspring of white settlers and slave women, those in the category of 'Mulattoes' were rarely allowed to inherit from their fathers but, in return, they were often liberated and educated. Up to this day, browns are associated with the liberal professions in these societies; in Jamaica, 'brown' is virtually a synonym for 'middle-class'. In the United States, on the contrary, the category of the Mulatto disappeared during the nineteenth century. Today, any individual who has the slightest phenotypical trace of African origin is classified as 'black'. So when a famous American professor in black history came to Trinidad in 1989 to give a lecture commemorating the 150th anniversary of the abolition of slavery, the Trinidadian audience was startled to discover that the man was nearly white. In the US, of course, he would have had no other choice than to define himself as black.

Indians in new worlds

With the arrival of Indian indentured labourers in some of the plantation colonies in the latter half of the nineteenth century, a new ethnic complexity developed. First of all, it is interesting here to note that the basis for the development of Indian ethnic identity was different from that of black identity. Although their economic and political situation was scarcely better than that of the slaves (Tinker, 1974), the Indians were free to form their own communities after migrating. As a result, important cultural practices were retained in their new worlds. Exaggerating somewhat, the Indo-Trinidadian author V.S. Naipaul (1969) has thus described rural Trinidad as a replication of rural Bihar (a state in north India). In some of these societies, notably in Mauritius, caste has continued to play an important part in social and political life.[2] Linguistic and cultural subdivisions which had been relevant in India, notably the Muslim–Hindu division and the division between speakers of Indo-European and speakers of Dravidian languages, were to some extent reproduced or refashioned. The latter distinction continues to exist in Mauritius, but not in Trinidad and Guyana. There are two complementary explanations for this. In Mauritius, unlike in the other societies which received indentured Indian labourers, a certain number of Tamils (Dravidians) had already arrived as free merchants during the period of slavery. There was thus a Tamil elite. Second, the Tamils were sufficiently numerous in Mauritius to be able to form effective career networks based on kinship and shared ethnic identity, and by the same token they were able to remain more or less endogamous.

In several of the societies which received large numbers of Indians, the blacks responded by strengthening their identity and ethnic boundaries. They developed stereotypes of Indians as backward, illiterate and pagan, and as a consequence many blacks began to reify and overcommunicate their own culture as more sophisticated, more up-to-date and sometimes more 'Europeanised' than that of the Indians, who were at the bottom of the social hierarchy. This kind of dynamic is a widespread aspect of hierarchical polyethnic systems. A group which is powerless undercommunicates its distinctiveness, but when the same group is in a superior position its members will overcommunicate it. This switch is frequently situational. The Coloured middle-class of nineteenth-century Trinidad, it has been said (Brereton, 1979), tended to be anti-racist upwards (vis-à-vis the whites) and racist downwards (vis-à-vis the blacks).

In order to understand the historical emergence of a particular ethnic configuration, we have seen repeatedly that it would be misleading to start from an assumption of 'primordial characteristics' of groups or categories. The formation of different categories of 'Indians' in Mauritius and Trinidad, respectively, clearly shows this. Not only are the ethnic subdivisions within the 'Indian' category

---

2 In Mauritius, caste divisions actually grew in political significance in the 1980s, following decades of political and economic modernisation.

different in the two societies, but so are the stereotypical assumptions about 'Indian culture'. Indians in Mauritius, where they are in a majority and dominate the state bureaucracy, often complain that they are good politicians but 'have no talent for business'. In Trinidad, Indians have a smaller stake in the state bureaucracy and many Indians have gone into business. Here, the common stereotype of self is exactly the opposite in this regard.

When we try to understand how and why particular forms of ethnic organisation have emerged in different societies, we must therefore ask not 'what are these people *really* like?' but rather, 'how are ethnic identifications created, and what purposes do they serve?'. Seen in this perspective, ethnicity as it can be identified in colonial and post-colonial societies with a capitalist mode of production must necessarily be very different from the kinds of categorisations which existed in pre-colonial times. The goals pursued by individuals are different, the relevant means for their achievement are different, and the encompassing social system is different. My description of plantation societies also indicates that ethnicity can be studied both as a phenomenon created by economic and political circumstances, and as a reaction to such circumstances. I shall now consider some further historical aspects of ethnogenesis in contexts of social and cultural change.

'Ethnic revitalisation': from people to a people

Following the integration of so-called traditional peoples into modern nation-states, symbolic universes merge in many respects. People become more similar in terms of practices and representations; an increasing part of their learnt capabilities for communication, their taken-for-granted structures of relevance – simply put, their *culture* – becomes shared. Under these circumstances people are more liable than before to reflect upon and objectify their way of life as *a* culture or as *a tradition*, and in this way they may become *a people* with an abstract sense of community and a presumed shared history. This kind of process has taken place among Trinidadians of Indian origin since the 1950s, but particularly since the economic growth associated with the oil boom of the 1970s (Vertovec, 1991; Eriksen, 1992b). Formerly, the 'East Indians' or Indo-Trinidadians were politically fragmented and had a poorly developed shared identity. They were villagers living off the land, with their extended kin group and their village as the most important foci for social organisation. In later years, education, the spread of modern mass media and social mobility have simultaneously integrated the mass of Indo-Trinidadians into a social system of larger scale than before, *and* increased their knowledge of the outside world. They have become consciously concerned with the preservation of 'their culture' and have formed organisations intended to pursue their cultural and political interests. Although the majority of Indo-Trinidadians no longer speak an Indian language, they are strongly oriented towards India in their search for roots and 'authentic culture'. Many middle-class Hindus in Trinidad have in recent years associated themselves with the charismatic Hinduist Sai Baba movement, which helps them to see their history as that of a dignified culture (Klass, 1991).

Most of the Indians who arrived in Trinidad as indentured labourers in the second half of the nineteenth century were rural low-caste people. The culture their descendants seek to 're-create', however, is largely Brahminic in character. Their ancestors in Bihar and Uttar Pradesh were villagers with no collective organisation and no social identity as 'Indians'. In other words, the presumed revitalisation of a half-forgotten ancestral culture turns out to be something qualitatively new – even if it is presented as old and time-honoured. The concept of 'Indian', as it is used in Trinidad, is a Trinidadian product.

It was formerly common to view contemporary ethnicity and 'tribalism' in Africa and elsewhere either as vestiges of the past or as forms of revitalisation, that is the re-emergence of identities and forms of organisation which had existed formerly but which had been on the verge of disappearance. More recent research has shown that this view, while it conforms to ethnic ideologies themselves (which are primordialist in that they stress continuity with the past as a *raison-d'être* for the unity of the ethnic group), tends to be misleading. Important aspects of such 'revitalisation movements' are entirely new, although they imagine themselves as old and glorify presumably ancient handicrafts, rituals or other cultural practices. The next example will illustrate this point clearly.

Colonialism and migration

The creation of plantation societies and the slave trade are well known aspects of colonialism. Somewhat less studied are the processes of social upheaval which took place in large parts of Africa in a later phase of colonialism, caused by the introduction of centralised state administration and a capitalist system of production. The state has integrated different groups into social systems of unprecedented scale. In many cases, this integration had only a superficial influence on people's daily lives. There are still, in the 1990s, many Africans who are for most practical purposes socially and culturally integrated at the village level.

In many other cases, however, capitalism and the state represented new systemic parameters with profound consequences for social organisation and individual life-paths. It is by virtue of these kinds of processes, many researchers have argued (for example A. Cohen, 1969; Worsley, 1984; O'Brien, 1986; Peel, 1989), that the contemporary ethnic identifications and boundaries were created. Categorical distinctions certainly existed before colonialism and capitalism, but perhaps 'the pocket in which they properly belong is part of a garment of an altogether different cut' (Fardon, 1987: 178). Notably, such categorisations were segmentary, fluid and less institutionalised than modern ethnic distinctions.

Drawing extensively on historical material as well as original fieldwork, Jay O'Brien (1986) has analysed the emergence of ethnic categorisations and groups in the Gezira area of the Sudan. The area was opened for irrigated cotton production in 1925, and it required the recruitment of large numbers of seasonal labourers during the peak season. The various groups or 'tribes' that recruited such labourers were integrated into the capitalist system of production in different ways because of differences in social organisation. However, the new ethnic categorisations, O'Brien argues, did not emerge from cultural differences but rather from variations in the form of integration in the capitalist system. Two examples illustrate this.

People from a variety of West African groups were recruited as cotton workers. They were all Muslims, and most could speak Hausa, but in other respects they were – and considered themselves as – culturally distinctive. These immigrants were accustomed to wagework and adapted easily to the conditions on the Gezira scheme, and the British frequently used them to replace locals who did not fulfil their obligations. Locally, the settlers were known under the generic term 'Fellata', which took on a basically pejorative meaning, with connotations of 'hard-working and slavish'. The settlers responded through a process of 'cultural realignment'. They began, collectively, to emphasise their distinctiveness vis-à-vis the locals, turning it into a virtue, and became Islamic fundamentalists in contrast to the slacker Muslims of the other categories. Gradually, they began to use the term 'Takari' for themselves, which is a respectful term for religious pilgrims from West Africa. In conclusion, O'Brien finds that 'partly in defensive adaptation to circumstances of discrimination and lumping together by others, these diverse cultural groups have drawn on commonalities of their past heritage and contemporary circumstances to forge a more or less coherent ethnic identity' (O'Brien, 1986: 903).

A different process of ethnic incorporation in the same area concerns the people now known as Joama' (O'Brien, 1986). They are Arabic speakers, Muslims and claim Arab origins. They had a reputation as reliable and hard-working labourers and were in high demand at the Gezira scheme, particularly from the 1950s. Their area of settlement became a prime recruiting ground for the cotton estates. Many job-seekers who were not Joama' thus began to settle near the Joama' area to facilitate their access to the labour market. Some of them would work as sharecroppers for the Joama' outside the cotton-picking season, and thus were gradually integrated into the Joama' social system. During fieldwork in 1977, O'Brien found that many families of non-Joama' origins were about to become assimilated. Some, who stated that they 'used to be Fellata', were already recognised as Joama', whereas others, in an earlier phase of assimilation, were seen as good workers who were 'just like the Joama''.

These analyses of different processes of ethnic incorporation show that the formation of ethnic identities in the Gezira came about through a specific intersection of existing local characteristics and the introduction of a capitalist system of production. Generalising further, O'Brien concludes that 'ethnicity as it has been encountered in the contemporary Third World ... has been constituted by the same world-historical process that has produced modern capitalism, wage labor, and class structures' (O'Brien, 1986: 905). Contemporary ethnicity, or 'tribalism', is not, in other words, a relic of the past but a product of modernisation processes leading up to the present. This point is supported further by a look at the semantics of ethnicity in contemporary Africa.

The semantics of ethnic labelling

It has frequently been remarked that many of the 'tribes' anthropologists have written about had no empirical existence outside the mind of the ethnographer (Southall, 1976; Kuper, 1988). Abstract loyalty to, and identification with, entities such as 'the Nuer' or 'the Dinka' were in many cases unthinkable for the agents themselves, whose main principles of organisation were kinship and locality. In many cases, even the actual names of 'tribes' were simply labels used by the colonial administration and were rarely or never used by the 'tribals' themselves. Thus the 'Yoruba', a major Nigerian tribe or ethnic group, is a twentieth-century phenomenon. Categorical labels with no social significance are likely to be unimportant, and in pre-colonial times many groups were politically organised along lines of kinship and personal loyalties and usually did not require categorical labels of greater scope. Epstein sees this when he writes, referring to Copperbelt material, that 'the term "tribe" did not carry the same meaning in the towns as it did in the rural areas; "tribalism" in urban and rural contexts related to phenomena of quite different orders' (Epstein, 1978: 10). This means that although ethnicity existed in pre-colonial times in Southern Africa, it took on a very different form from that which it does today. Complex modern societies seem to imply processes of identity and boundary maintenance which are much more acutely felt, and more self-consciously fashioned, than has been the case in other kinds of societies.

In a critique of the most generalising uses of the term ethnicity, Richard Fardon (1987) gives an account of the development of Chamba ethnicity which shows that today's ethnic categorisations can have historical precedents which were quite different in their social functioning.

The Chamba are presently considered, and consider themselves, a people or an ethnic group. They number around a quarter of a million and live on both sides of the Nigeria–Cameroon border. The western and eastern Chamba speak different languages, which may belong to different classes, while the central Chamba 'were formed by the fusion of speakers of the two languages' (Fardon, 1987: 179). It seems likely that intermingling between the groups, followed by the formation of Chamba chiefdoms in the nineteenth century, account for the present distributions of Chamba peoples.

Even today, different categories of Chamba, and members of the same categories in different situations, use four different terms of self-identification which distinguish them from different categories of others, both within and outside of 'the Chamba group'. The word Chamba itself derives from one of these four categorisations, Sama or Samba, and as an identity tag it 'became ... absolute only after the establishment of the colonial and then the national state' (Fardon, 1987: 181). Further, there were formerly important distinctions based on contrasts between chiefly and priestly sections in the communities, as well as the ubiquitous distinctions based on lineage.

Fardon's conclusion is that 'the Chamba did not exist in the nineteenth century, not just because [the term] Chamba describes people whose origins, languages and cultures are diverse ... but because ethnic entities which have the form of the modern Chamba ethnicity are modern inventions' (Fardon, 1987: 182).

A related but more general point concerning the historical emergence of ethnic labels is stated forcefully in Edwin Ardener's short essay 'Language, ethnicity and population' (Ardener, 1989a [1972]). In this rather dense and pyrotechnic exposition, Ardener first relativises the significance of contemporary and colonial ethnic labels by showing that they scarcely correspond to pre-colonial identities. He then argues that they function in a recursive way, since the labels used by colonisers, missionaries and foreign scholars were returned to and appropriated by the people in question. Finally, Ardener divorces ethnicity altogether from demography by showing that there does not have to be biological continuity among the carriers of a particular ethnic label. The linguistic and ethnic category of 'Kole', he argues, 'may have been filled according to different criteria at different times' (Ardener, 1989a [1972]: 69) — in other words, people classified as 'Kole' were recruited from other groups according to varying principles.

Ardener's theoretical points concerning ethnic labelling are as follows:

1. The ethnic classification is a reflex of self-identification.
2. Onomastic (or naming) propensities are closely involved in this, and thus have more than a purely linguistic interest.
3. Identification by others is an important feature in the establishment of self-identification.
4. The taxonomic space in which self-identification occurs is of overriding importance.
5. The effect of foreign classification, 'scientific' and lay, is far from neutral in the establishment of such a space. (Ardener, 1989a [1972]: 68)

Fardon, Southall and Ardener are all concerned with the semantics of ethnicity – with the introduction of and use of names in the conceptual reification of groups. A shared assumption is that groups tend to be fluid and segmentary in character and that boundaries between them are fuzzy, ambiguous and situational. The establishment of clear labels for large categories of people may thus have a conceptually, but also socially reifying effect on groups as they become official names and their members start using them in their self-identification. As we shall see in the next chapter, the same kind of processes are at work in nationalist movements.

The mere act of naming a smaller or larger cluster of clans, villages or lineages with a collective label is not, of course, sufficient to turn the discrete and fluid groups into ethnic categories. Fardon connects the emergence of Chamba ethnicity with the development of centralised (colonial) state administration, but also notes that other writers have 'given prominence to the economic conditions associated with the spread of capitalist organization of production and marketing'. He attributes this difference to variations between societies: his material deals with 'an economically underdeveloped area of west Africa, whereas emphasis upon economic factors occurs in analyses of southern Africa' (Fardon, 1987: 178). Studies of changes in the semantics of ethnicity are thus complementary to studies of more general processes of social and cultural change such as those discussed earlier in this chapter. Before looking more closely into some such processes in the contemporary world in chapters 6 and 7, we shall consider the consequences of mass education and the introduction of new communication technologies.

Modern education and ethnic identity

Technology can be essential in generating opportunities and constraints for culture and social organisation. Most of the complex, large-scale societies we know would probably have been less effectively integrated without effective communication technology. Mass education, which entails the spreading of books and other texts which describe and reify history and culture, plays an important part in this respect.

Uniform educational systems covering large areas greatly facilitate the development of abstract identifications with a category of people whom one will never meet – who are neither kinsfolk, nor affines nor neighbours (for example 'the Chamba' or 'the Kole'). It enables a large number of people to learn, simultaneously, which ethnic group they belong to and what are the cultural characteristics of that group. Standardised mass education can therefore be an extremely powerful machine for the creation of abstract identifications. Literacy enables people to create 'authorised' versions of their history, and in view of the 'objective' status granted written accounts of history in most literate societies (cf. Lévi-Strauss, 1962: ch. 9, for a depiction of history as myth), the manipulation, selection or reinterpretation of history for political or other purposes becomes an important activity in the creation and re-creation of ethnic allegiances.

In this way, mass education can be an efficient aid in the establishment of standardised reifications of culture, which are essential in the legitimation of ethnic identities. Mass-produced accounts of 'our people' or 'our culture' are important tools in the fashioning of an ethnic identity with a presumed cultural continuity in time.

As Lévi-Strauss has emphasised, illiterate people are no less capable of forming abstractions than the literate, but the kinds of abstraction created in illiterate societies are of a different order: they can be described as the 'science of the concrete' (Lévi-Strauss, 1962: ch. 1; cf. Comaroff and Comaroff, 1992: ch. 2). Similarly, Benedict Anderson would argue two decades later, all communities beyond the size of a closed village are abstractly imagined by their members, but the *style* of imagination differs. Anderson singles out modern imagined communities, in particular nations, as distinctive and unique – largely because they have arisen in the age of 'print-capitalism' (Anderson, 1991 [1983]; cf. Goody, 1977; cf. also chapter 6).

Ethnicity, history and culture

Several of the anthropological perspectives on ethnicity presented so far ignore the possible ways in which *cultural* peculiarities may give shape to ethnicity. In fact, many important studies of ethnicity – from the contributions to Barth (1969b), Abner Cohen (1974b) and Despres (1975b) to Rex and Mason (1986), Nash (1988), Fardon (1987) and others, seem to argue that culture and cultural variation are irrelevant in the study of ethnicity. What is usually the focus of enquiry is the way in which 'real or imagined' cultural differences assume social importance, and it has become a standard procedure for anthropologists to polemicise against the 'misplaced concreteness' involved in reifications of culture, whether they are undertaken by natives or by anthropologists. It has been repeatedly stressed that ethnic identities, groups and beliefs of shared culture and history are *creations* – whether they are created by historical circumstances, by strategic actors or as unintended consequences of political projects. Ethnic identities based on assumptions of shared culture may thus appear as 'accidents of history' (Leach's phrase) and little more. As Ardener has so eloquently argued, ethnic groups can profitably be regarded as self-defining entities: 'Ethnicities demand to be viewed from the inside. They have no imperative relationship with particular "objective" criteria' (Ardener, 1989b [1974]: 111). As numerous studies have shown, history, including 'emic' ethnohistory of the kind discussed in chapter 4, is written in the present and expresses present concerns (cf. Tonkin *et al.*, 1989). Thus the work of historians, lay or professional, may ultimately be equated with informants' statements by this kind of anthropological perspective.

An extreme version of this argument would lead to pure constructivism. Granted that ethnic categorisations and group formations are the results of historical contingencies, and granted that the history documenting the existence of a certain ethnic group can be written in virtually any way regardless of what really happened in the past, one seems forced to conclude that 'anything goes' – that *any* ethnic identity is imaginable, regardless of actual cultural variation or proveable distinctive origins. The fact that ethnic categories like Chamba, Joama' and Afro-Caribbean have come into being has no intrinsic relationship to any shared cultural characteristics initially possessed by the members of these categories. In sum, we may suggest, with Ernest Renan, that nationhood (or ethnic identity) involves shared memories, but also a great deal of shared forgetting (Renan 1992 [1882].

This kind of argument has clearly been indispensable (and it pervades much of the anthropological literature on ethnicity), but it leaves important questions unanswered. Obviously, it would have been impossible to persuade Chamba that they were really Yoruba, or to convince English people that they belonged to the same ethnic category as Chinese. At the least, such categorisations seem very, very far off. It seems clear, therefore, that the construction of ethnic categories takes place within a defined space and that some new categorisations may be viable while others are not. The question is: can such a space be defined in terms of cultural variation at all? The answer is, probably, that this is sometimes possible, but not always.

In a series of books on nationalism, A.D. Smith (see in particular A.D. Smith, 1986) argues that modern ethnic ideologies, notably nationalisms, have identifiable 'objective' cultural roots. He claims that the cultural continuity with the past which is emphasised by ethnic ideologists and national historians is not all make-believe and manipulative invention of the past. In effect, he argues that there *is* such a cultural continuity with the past, although the nations and ethnic movements themselves are modern creations. In many cases it is clear that group history has been fashioned so as to serve present needs, but this does not imply that anything goes. There are only so many plausible versions of history.

Concerning the construction of national ethnic identity in Norway, for example (cf. chapter 6), the number of options available in the mid-nineteenth century for western Norwegian nationalists were limited: they could effectively choose between a western Norwegian, a Norwegian, a Dano-Norwegian, and a Scandinavian identity. This was partly due to political circumstances, but also to the fact that the people involved would scarcely identify themselves as members of an ethnic nation containing people to whom they felt culturally unrelated.

Anthropology has a strong bias towards studying the present – and in their dealings with the past many anthropologists regard it as neither more nor less than present-day constructions of the past. Some anthropologists, among them Wolf and Worsley, have stressed the need of understanding the past in order to understand the present – and by this, they mean understanding what really took place, not what present-day informants or historians claim took place. O'Brien's work in the Sudan, which was summarised earlier in this chapter, should exemplify that it may be worthwhile to study history *as such*, and not just as a present-day rationalisation or part of an ideological justification for would-be ethnic leaders (although the latter aspect is also highly relevant).

Cultural history in ethnic identity

Arguing explicitly against those studies of ethnicity which ignore cultural history and cultural factors generally, John Peel (1989) offers an interpretation of Yoruba ethnicity in historical perspective. He admits, referring to Abner Cohen's work in Ibadan, that there may be compelling political reasons for ethnic mobilisation. He also concedes, referring to Maryon McDonald's work in Brittany (McDonald, 1989; cf. chapter 6), that the creative fashioning (or invention) of 'ethnohistory' among intellectuals has been an important technique for the creation of that abstract group consciousness among the masses which we think of as ethnic identity. However, Peel says, 'despite the "invention of tradition" that [the writing of ethnohistory] may involve, unless it also makes genuine contact with people's actual experience, that is with *a history that happened*, it is not likely to be effective' (Peel, 1989: 200, my emphasis). Nothing comes out of nothing, in other words.

Along with the Hausa and the Igbo, the Yoruba is one of Nigeria's 'mega-tribal' groupings, with more members than there are citizens in many nation-states. As such it is entirely a modern category, since the great-grandparents of most of the people who today identify themselves as Yoruba did not identify themselves in such a way. In other words, the parallel with the other African examples discussed in this chapter is evident. At the beginning of the twentieth century, the Yoruba were identical with what is today one Yoruba grouping, the Oyo. Like the Joama' of the Sudan, this ethnic category was vastly expanded as other groups took on Yoruba identity from the 1920s onwards, following migration, cash-cropping, education and conversion to world religions, creating a Nigeria-wide system of communication and exchange. From the late 1930s modern Yoruba political organisation, dichotomised against a similar Igbo organisation, began to develop. Thus Peel concords with the 'constructionist' argument on the modern character of ethnicity by stating that administrative units (regions and states) have in important ways contributed to shaping ethnic organisation. However, he also stresses that this has been a two-way process, mediated by politics, where the ethnic groups themselves have played an important part too. It is certainly no accident that the main divisions in Nigerian politics follow ethnic boundaries, and Peel connects this to cultural differences and identifications which were intrinsically related to pre-colonial experiences.

In order to document this connection with the past, he draws extensively on historical accounts.

The peoples who would later come to know themselves as Yoruba would in pre-colonial times recognise their affinity with others through shared language and/or shared customs. Since customs were to a great extent shared with members of other groups, language eventually became the most important vessel for Yoruba identity. This language-based identity was codified and spread in two principal ways: through liberated Yoruba slaves in diasporas (particularly in Sierra Leone) and through the work of missions, which played a pivotal part in creating a written Yoruba language. The missions were successful in this part of Nigeria, and during the latter half of the nineteenth century Yoruba identity came to be associated with Christianity. A local scholar called Samuel Johnson even fashioned a version of Yoruba history, completed in 1899 but published only in 1921, which 'proved' that the Yoruba were descendants of Coptic Christians from Upper Egypt. In this way, the recent paganism was depicted as an unfortunate interlude. In addition, wars with other groups, notably the Fulani, strengthened the feeling of a shared destiny and sharpened boundaries.

Paradoxically, Ibadan, the main Yoruba city, was to become a predominantly Muslim city. Although Yoruba cultural history is strongly associated with early conversion to Christianity, the modern Yoruba group is divided between Christianity and Islam. Moreover, the Muslim Yoruba are identified as the 'Yoruba proper' (the Oyo), whereas the Christians are regarded as 'adopted Yoruba'. Due to this 'fault-line' dividing the community (and several other Nigerian ethnic categories) along religious lines, religion cannot be used as a marker of ethnic identity. This ethnic 'pan-Yoruba' identity is nevertheless evident in both groups, although they do not always function as a political group. Yoruba segments, whether Christian or Muslim, or in alliances with Igbo or Hausa, remain Yoruba by virtue of their cultural identity.

The material presented by Peel is reminiscent of Fardon's and Ardener's accounts of ethnogenesis in neighbouring areas, as he links the development of contemporary ethnic identity and organisation to the same kind of modernisation processes that the other authors cite. However, Peel's conclusions are different in that he emphasises not the ways in which the present has shaped the past, but the ways in which the past has shaped the present. Arguing rather pointedly against the 'presentism' dominating social anthropology, he targets in particular Abner Cohen's assumption that ethnicity requires neither a cultural nor a historical explanation, but can be reduced to politics and contemporary 'structural conditions'. Against Cohen, Peel argues the need to take historical accounts seriously – both as sources documenting actual events more or less accurately, and as serious attempts by 'natives' to come to terms with their past. Ethnohistory should not, in his view, simply be regarded as a technique to generate a particular present, but can also be taken seriously at its face value – as an expression of an interest in the past.

This point is important. Together with the kind of history Wolf, Worsley and O'Brien recommend for scrutiny – economic and political history – the cultural histories of peoples may certainly shed light on the origins of contemporary ethnicity, and should not be seen merely as aspects of the present. Two main concerns in the anthropological study of ethnic identity and organisation have been to reveal ethnohistory as ideology fashioned to satisfy contemporary needs (as discussed in chapter 4), and to point out that there is no necessary fit between ethnic discontinuities and discontinuities of 'objective culture', respectively. This kind of argument leaves important questions unanswered. We may nevertheless ask, with Peel, whether anthropologists are really trained to ask questions relating to history seen as the past and not just as justifications for present concerns. Peel writes:

The present has often been treated by anthropologists as a kind of temporal plateau, coterminous with the duration of their fieldwork, inhabited by structures and categories; but it is much more evanescent than that, no sooner come than gone, really no more than the hinge between the past and future. (Peel, 1989: 213)

The issue he takes on is much too vast for us to go into here. Many anthropologists would be inclined to argue against claims to the effect that identities *are* continuous through time. Perhaps they only *seem* continuous and our analytical task consists in showing that they are not, and that the very notion that people ought be concerned with the past is an ideological child of the age of nationalism. In this perspective, one might argue that while trees have roots, humans don't – and that any claim to the effect that humans need roots is ideological. As a way of examining this and related questions in greater detail, we now turn to a closer investigation of nationalism, thereby bringing the anthropological study of ethnicity even closer to home than we have done so far.

6 NATIONALISM

Nationalism is not the awakening of nations to self-consciousness: it invents nations where they do not exist.

Ernest Gellner (1964: 169)

—But do you know what a nation means? says John Wyse.
—Yes, says Bloom.
—What is it? says John Wyse.
—A nation? says Bloom. A nation is the same people living in the same place.
—By God, then, says Ned, laughing, if that's so I'm a nation for I'm living in the same place for the past five years.
So of course everyone had a laugh at Bloom and says he, trying to muck out of it:
—Or also living in different places.
—That covers my case, says Joe.

James Joyce (1984: 329–30)

The race to nation[1]

For years, anthropological studies of ethnicity concentrated on relationships between groups which were of such a size that they could be studied through our traditional field methods: participant observation, personal interviews and surveys. The empirical focus of anthropological studies was almost by default a local community. If the state was given consideration, it would usually be as a part of the wider context, for instance as an external agent influencing local conditions. Besides, anthropology was traditionally biased towards the study of 'remote others'. As argued earlier, the general shift in

---

1 This pun was stolen from Brackette Williams' essay 'A class act: anthropology and the race to nation across ethnic terrain' (B. Williams, 1989).

terminology from 'tribe' to 'ethnic group' relativises such an Us/Them dichotomy, since ethnic groups, unlike 'tribes', obviously exist among 'ourselves' as well as among the 'others'. The boundary mechanisms that keep ethnic groups more or less discrete have the same formal characteristics in a London suburb as in the New Guinea highlands, and the development of ethnic identity can be studied with largely the same conceptual tools in New Zealand as in Central Europe – although the empirical contexts are distinctive and ultimately unique. This has today been acknowledged in social anthropology, where perhaps a majority of researchers now study complex 'unbounded' systems rather than supposedly isolated communities.

Nationalism is a new topic for anthropology. The study of nationalism – the ideology of the modern nation-state – was for many years left to political scientists, macrosociologists and historians. Nations and nationalist ideologies are definitely modern large-scale phenomena. However, although the study of nationalism raises methodological problems relating to scale and the impossibility of isolating the unit of study, these problems inevitably arise in relation to other topics as well. Social changes have taken place in the traditional heartlands of anthropological research, integrating millions of people into markets and states. Like ourselves, our informants are citizens. Further, 'primitive societies' probably never were as isolated as was formerly held, and they were no more 'pristine' and 'original' than our own societies (Wolf, 1982). Indeed, as Adam Kuper (1988) has shown, the very idea of primitive society was a European invention which emerged under particular historical circumstances.

An early but largely neglected venture into the anthropological study of nation-states was Lloyd Fallers' (1974) research in Uganda and Turkey, where he explicitly tried to link data from both micro and macro levels in his analyses (cf. also Gluckman, 1961; Grønhaug, 1974). However, the study of nationalism has truly become a topic within anthropology only during the 1980s and 1990s.

In the classic terminology of social anthropology, the term 'nation' was used in an inaccurate way to designate large categories of people or societies with more or less uniform culture. In his introductory textbook, I.M. Lewis (1985: 287) states: 'By the term nation, following the best anthropological authority we understand, of course, a culture-unit.' Later, Lewis makes it clear that he sees no reason for distinguishing between 'tribes', 'ethnic groups' and 'nations', since the difference appears to be one of size, not of structural composition or functioning. Comparing groups of several million with smaller segments, he asks: 'Are these smaller segments significantly different?

My answer is that they are not: that they are simply smaller units of the same kind ...' (Lewis, 1985: 358).

In this chapter, I shall argue that it can indeed be worthwhile to distinguish nations from ethnic categories because of their relationship to a modern state. It will also be shown that an anthropological perspective is essential for a full understanding of nationalism. An analytical and empirical focus on nationalism can further be illuminating in research on modernisation and social change, as well as being highly relevant for the wider fields of political anthropology and the study of social identities.

What is nationalism?

Ernest Gellner begins his famous book on nationalism by defining the concept like this:

Nationalism is primarily a political principle, which holds that the political and the national unit should be congruent.

Nationalism as a sentiment, or as a movement, can best be defined in terms of this principle. Nationalist *sentiment* is the feeling of anger aroused by the violation of the principle, or the feeling of satisfaction aroused by its fulfilment. A nationalist *movement* is one actuated by sentiment of this kind. (Gellner, 1983: 1; cf. Gellner, 1978: 134)

While this definition at first glance may seem a straightforward one, it turns out to be circular. For what is the 'national unit'? Gellner goes on to explain that he sees it as synonymous with an ethnic group – or at least an ethnic group which the nationalists claim exists: 'In brief, nationalism is a theory of political legitimacy, which requires that ethnic boundaries should not cut across political ones' (Gellner, 1983: 1). In other words, nationalism, the way the term is used by Gellner and other contemporary social scientists, refers to a peculiar link between ethnicity and the state. Nationalisms are, in this view, ethnic ideologies which hold that their group should dominate a state. A nation-state, therefore, is a state dominated by an ethnic group, whose markers of identity (such as language or religion) are frequently embedded in its official symbolism and legislation.

In another important theoretical study of nationalism, Benedict Anderson proposes the following definition of the nation: 'it is an imagined political community – and imagined as both inherently limited and sovereign' (Anderson, 1991 [1983]: 6). By 'imagined', he does not necessarily mean 'invented', but rather that people who define themselves as members of a nation 'will never know most of their fellow-members, meet them, or even hear of them, yet in the minds of each lives the image of their communion' (ibid.). Unlike Gellner and many others, who concentrate on the political aspects of nationalism, Anderson is concerned to understand the force and persistence of national identity and sentiment. The fact that people are willing to die for their nation, he notes, indicates its extraordinary force.

Despite this difference in emphasis, Anderson's perspective is largely compatible with Gellner's. Both stress that nations are ideological constructions seeking to forge a link between (self-defined) cultural group and state, and that they create abstract communities of a different order from those dynastic states or kinship-based communities which pre-dated them.

The main task Anderson sets himself is to provide an explanation for what he calls the 'anomaly of nationalism'. According to both Marxist and liberal social theories of modernisation, nationalism should not have been viable in an individualist post-Enlightenment world, referring as it does to 'primordial loyalties' and solidarity based on common origins and culture. In particular, Anderson notes with a certain puzzlement that socialist states tend to be nationalist in character. 'The reality is quite plain,' he writes, 'the 'end of the era of nationalism', so long prophesied, is not remotely in sight. Indeed, nation-ness is the most universally legitimate value in the political life of our time' (Anderson, 1991 [1983], 3).

Anthropological research on ethnic boundaries and identity processes could help to illuminate Anderson's *problematique*. Research on ethnic identity formation and boundary maintenance has indicated that ethnic identities tend to attain their greatest importance in situations of flux, change, resource competition and threats against boundaries. It is not surprising, therefore, that political movements based on cultural identity are strong in societies undergoing modernisation, although this does not account for the fact that these movements become *nationalist* movements.

The remarkable congruence between theories of nationalism and anthropological theory of ethnicity seems unrecognised (or at least unacknowledged) by Gellner and Anderson. Since the two bodies of theory have largely developed independently of each other, I shall point out the main parallels.

Both studies of ethnicity at the local community level and studies of nationalism at the state level stress that ethnic or national identities are constructions; they are not 'natural'. Moreover, the link between a particular identity and the 'culture' it seeks to reify is not a one-to-one relationship. Widespread assumptions of congruence between ethnicity and 'objective culture' are in both cases shown to be cultural constructions themselves. *Talk about culture* and *culture* can here, perhaps, be distinguished in roughly the same way as one distinguishes between the menu and the food. They are social facts of different orders.

When we look at nationalism, the link between ethnic organisation and ethnic identity discussed earlier becomes crystal-clear. According to nationalism, the political organisation should be ethnic in character in that it represents the interests of a particular ethnic group. Conversely, the nation-state draws an important aspect of its political legitimacy from convincing the popular masses that it really does represent them as a cultural unit.

An emphasis on the duality of meaning and politics, common in ethnicity studies as well as research on nationalism, can also be related to anthropological theory on ritual symbols. In his work on the Ndembu, Victor Turner (1967; 1969) has showed that these symbols are multivocal and that they have an 'instrumental' and a 'sensory' (or meaningful) pole. In a remarkably parallel way, Anderson argues that nationalism derives its force from its combination of political legit-imation and emotional power. Abner Cohen (1974b) has argued along similar lines when he states that politics cannot be purely instrumental, but must always involve symbols which have the power of creating loyalty and a feeling of belongingness.

Anthropologists who have written about nationalism have generally seen it as a variant of ethnicity. I shall also do this to begin with; later on, I shall nevertheless raise the question of whether *non-ethnic nation-alisms* are imaginable.

The nation as a cultural community

Both Gellner and Anderson emphasise that although nations tend to imagine themselves as old, they are modern. Nationalist ideology was first developed in Europe and in European diaspora (particularly in the New World; cf. Handler and Segal, 1992) in the period around the French Revolution. Here we must distinguish between *tradition* and *traditionalism*. Nationalism, which is frequently a traditionalis-tic ideology, may glorify and recodify an ostensibly ancient tradition shared by the ancestors of the members of the nation, but it does not thereby re-create that tradition. It *reifies* it in the same way that the Hurons reified their supposed tradition (see chapter 4).

Since nationalism is a modern phenomenon which has unfolded in the full light of recorded history, the 'ethnogenesis' of nations lends itself more easily to investigation than the history of non-modern peoples. Thus the creation of Norwegian national identity took place throughout the nineteenth century, which was a period of modernisation and urbanisation. The country moved to full independence, leaving the union with Sweden, in 1905.

Early Norwegian nationalism mainly derived its support from the urban middle classes. Members of the city bourgeoisie travelled to remote valleys in search of 'authentic Norwegian culture', brought elements from it back to the city and presented them as the authentic expression of Norwegianness. Folk costumes, painted floral patterns (*rosemaling*), traditional music and peasant food became national symbols even to people who had not grown up with such customs. Actually it was the city dwellers, not the peasants, who decided that reified aspects of peasant culture should be 'the national culture'. A national heroic history was established. The creation of 'national arts', which were markers of uniqueness and sophistication, was also an important part of the nationalist project in Norway as elsewhere. Typical representatives of this project were the composer Edvard Grieg, who incorporated local folk tunes into his Romantic scores, and the author Bjørnstjerne Bjørnson, whose peasant tales were widely read.

Certain aspects of peasant culture were thus reinterpreted and placed into an urban political context as 'evidence' that Norwegian culture was distinctive, that Norwegians were 'a people' and that they therefore ought to have their own state. This national symbolism was efficient in raising ethnic boundaries vis-à-vis Swedes and Danes, and simultaneously it emphasised that urban and rural Norwegians belonged to the same culture and had shared political interests. This idea of urban–rural solidarity, characteristic of nationalism, was, as Gellner has pointed out, a political innovation. Before the age of nationalism, the ruling classes were usually cosmopolitan in character. Anderson writes with a certain glee (1991 [1983]: 83n) that up to the First World War no 'English' dynasty had ruled England since the mid-eleventh century. Furthermore, the idea that the aristocracy belonged to the same culture as the peasants must have seemed abominable to the former and incomprehensible to the latter before nationalism.

Nationalism stresses solidarity between the poor and the rich, between the propertyless and the capitalists. According to nationalist ideology, the sole principle of political exclusion and inclusion follows the boundaries of the nation – that category of people defined as members of the same culture.

The political use of cultural symbols

The example of Norwegian nationalism indicates the 'inventedness' of the nation. Until the late nineteenth century, Norway's main written language had been Danish. It was partly replaced by a new literary language, *Nynorsk* or 'New Norwegian', based on Norwegian dialects. Vernacularisation is an important aspect of many nationalist movements, since a shared language can be a powerful symbol of cultural unity as well as a convenient tool in the administration of a nation-state. When it comes to culture, it could be argued that urban Norwegians in Christiania (today's Oslo) and Bergen had more in common with urban Swedes and Danes than with rural Norwegians. Indeed, the spoken language in these cities is still, in the 1990s, closer to standard Danish than to some rural dialects. Further, the selection of symbols to be used in the nation's representation of itself was highly politically motivated. In many cases, the so-called ancient, typically Norwegian customs, folk tales, handicrafts and so on were neither ancient, typical nor Norwegian. The painted floral patterns depict grapevines from the Mediterranean. The Hardanger fiddle music and most of the folk tales had their origin in Central Europe, and many of the 'typical folk costumes' which are worn at public celebrations such as Constitution Day were designed by nationalists early in the twentieth century. Most of the customs depicted as typical came from specific mountain valleys in southern Norway.

When such practices are reified as symbols and transferred to a nationalist discourse, their meaning changes. The use of presumedly typical ethnic symbols in nationalism is intended to stimulate reflection on one's own cultural distinctiveness and thereby to create a feeling of nationhood. Nationalism reifies culture in the sense that it enables people to talk about their culture as though it were a constant. In Richard Handler's accurate phrase, nationalist discourses are 'attempts to construct bounded cultural objects' (Handler, 1988: 27). The ethnic boundary mechanisms discussed earlier are evident here, as well as inventive uses of history which create an impression of continuity. When Norway became independent, its first king was recruited from the Danish royal family. He was nevertheless named Haakon VII as a way of stressing the (entirely fictional) continuity with the dynasty of kings that ruled Norway before 1350.

The discrepancy between national ideology (comprising symbols, stereotypes and the like) and social practice is no less apparent in the case of nations than with respect to other ethnic groups. However, as Anderson diplomatically remarks, every community based on wider links than face-to-face contact is imagined, and nations are neither more nor less 'fraudulent' than other communities. We have earlier seen similar identity processes in discussions of other ethnic groups; what is peculiar to nationalism is its relationship to the state. With the help of the powers of the nation-state, nations can be invented where they do not exist, to paraphrase Gellner (1964). Standardisation of language, the creation of national labour markets based on individual labour contracts and compulsory schooling, which presuppose the prior existence of a nation-state, gradually forge nations out of diverse human material. Thus, while it would have been impossible a hundred years ago to state exactly where Norwegian dialects merged into Swedish dialects, this linguistic boundary is now more clear-cut and follows the political one.[2]

The earlier, dynastic states in Europe placed few demands on the majority of their citizens (Birch, 1989), and they did not require cultural uniformity in society. It did not matter that the serfs spoke a different language from that of the rulers, or that the serfs in one region spoke a different language from those in another region. Why is the standardisation of culture so important in modern nation-states?

Nationalism and industrial society

Gellner, Ralph Grillo (1980) and others have argued that nationalist ideology emerged as a reaction to industrialisation and the uprooting of people from their local communities. Industrialisation entailed great geographic mobility, and a vast number of people became participants in the same economic (and later the same political) system. Kinship ideology, feudalism and religion were no longer capable of organising people efficiently.

In addition, the new industrial system of production required the facility to replace workers on a large scale. Thus workers had to have many of the same skills and capabilities. Industrialisation implied the need for a standardisation of skills, a kind of process which can also be described as 'cultural homogenisation'. Mass education is instrumental in this homogenising process. By introducing national consciousness to every nook and cranny of the country, it turns 'peasants into Frenchmen' (Weber, 1976).

In this historical context, a need arises for a new kind of ideology capable of creating cohesion and loyalty among individuals participating in social systems on a huge scale. Nationalism was able to satisfy these requirements. It postulated the existence of an imagined community based on shared culture and embedded in the state, where people's loyalty and attachment should be directed towards

---

2 Swedish, Danish and Norwegian are closely related languages. We owe the fact that they are considered three distinctive ones and not variants of a shared Scandinavian language to nationalism.

the state and the legislative system rather than towards members of their kin group or village. In this way, nationalist ideology is functional for the state.

Its political effectiveness is one condition for nationalist ideology to be viable; it must refer to a nation which can be embodied in a nation-state and effectively ruled. An additional condition is popular support. What does nationalism then have to offer? As some of the examples below will suggest, nationalism offers security and perceived stability at a time when life-worlds are fragmented and people are being uprooted. An important aim of nationalist ideology is thus to re-create a sentiment of wholeness and continuity with the past; to transcend that alienation or rupture between individual and society that modernity has brought about.

At the identity level, nationhood is a matter of belief. The nation, that is the *Volk* imagined by nationalists, is a product of nationalist ideology; it is not the other way around. A nation exists from the moment a handful of influential people decide that it should be so, and it starts, in most cases, as an urban elite phenomenon. In order to be an efficient political tool, it must nevertheless eventually achieve mass appeal.

Communications technology and nationhood

One important difference between nations and other kinds of community, including many ethnic communities, concerns scale. With a few exceptions (notably mini-states in the Caribbean and the Pacific), nation-states are social systems operating on a vast scale. Tribal societies and other local communities could to a great extent rely on kinship networks and face-to-face interaction for their maintenance as systems and for the loyalty of their members. Even in the great dynastic states, most of the subjects were locally integrated; they were first and foremost members of families and villages. Socialisation and social control were largely handled locally. Armies tended to be professional, unlike in nationalist societies, where it is considered the moral duty of all to fight for their country.

Nations are communities where the citizens are expected to be integrated in respect to culture and self-identity in an abstract, anonymous manner. One of Anderson's most telling illustrations of this abstract character of the moral community of the nation is the tomb of the Unknown Soldier. Usually these tombs are left deliberately empty; they signify the universal, abstract character of the nation. 'Yet void as these tombs are of identifiable mortal remains or immortal souls, they are nonetheless saturated with ghostly *national* imaginings' (Anderson, 1991 [1983]: 9).

What are the conditions for such an abstract ideology? I have described the economic and political concomitants of nationalism, and here we shall add a technological prerequisite for it, namely communications technology facilitating the standardisation of knowledge or representations (cf. chapter 5). Anderson strongly emphasises print-capitalism as an important condition for nationalism. Through the spread of the printed word in cheap editions, a potentially unlimited number of persons have access to identical information without direct contact with the originator.

More recently, newspapers, television and radio have played – and still play – a crucial part in standardising representations and language. These media also play an important part in the reproduction and strengthening of nationalist sentiments. During the Falklands/Malvinas war in 1982, for example, the British media depicted the war quite consistently as a 'simple opposition between good and evil' (J. Taylor, 1992: 30), whereas the Argentinian media depicted it as a struggle against colonialism (Caistor, 1992).

A different kind of communications technology might also be considered here, namely modern means of transportation. In the mid-nineteenth century, it could take a week to cross Trinidad; today, the journey takes little more than an hour. Modern transportation technology greatly facilitates the integration of people into larger social systems, increasing the flow of people and goods indefinitely. It creates conditions for the integration of people into nation-states, and in this way it may have important indirect effects at the level of consciousness in making people *feel* that they are members of the nation.

A metaphor appropriate to the political and cultural developments leading to nationalism is the map. Although maps existed before nationalism, the map can be a very concise and potent symbol of the nation. Country maps, present in classrooms all over the world, depict the nation simultaneously as a bounded, observable thing and as an abstraction of something which has a physical reality. Most world maps place Europe at the centre of the world. This is not a politically innocent act!

Most students of nationalism emphasise its modern and abstract aspects. Anthropological perspectives are particularly valuable here, since anthropologists may throw into relief the unique and peculiar character of nationalism and nation-states through comparisons with small-scale societies. In this perspective, the nation and nationalist ideology appear at least partly as symbolic tools for the ruling classes in societies which would otherwise have been threatened by potential dissolution. Some writers have argued that nationalism and national communities can have profound roots in earlier ethnic communities or *ethnies* (A.D. Smith, 1986), but it would be misleading to claim that there is an unbroken continuity from the pre-modern communities or 'cultures' to the national ones. As the Norwegian example shows, folk costumes and other national symbols take on a very different meaning in the modern context from that which they originally had.

Nationalism as religion and metaphoric kinship

Nationalism in itself belongs neither on the left nor on the right of the political spectrum. Through an emphasis on equality between citizens, it may be an ideology of the left. By emphasising vertical solidarity and the exclusion of foreigners, it may belong on the right. Anderson suggests that nationalism (as well as other ethnic ideologies) should be classified together with kinship and religion rather than with fascism and liberalism (Anderson, 1991: 15). It is an ideology which proclaims that the *Gemeinschaft* threatened by mass society can survive through a concern with roots and cultural continuity.

In a study of the nationalisms of Sri Lanka and Australia, Bruce Kapferer (1988; 1989) describes nationalism as an *ontology*; that is a doctrine about the essence of reality. Through his examples from the two very different societies, Kapferer shows how nationalism can instil passions and profound emotions in its followers. It frequently draws on religion and myth for its symbolism, which is often violent in character. (One needs only to think of military parades, which are common in the celebration of Independence Days in many countries.) Like other ethnic ideologies, nationalism lays claim to symbols which have great importance for people, and argues that these symbols represent the nation-state. Death is often important in nationalist symbolism: individuals who have died in war are depicted as martyrs who died in defence of their nation. If the nation is a community that one is willing to die for, reasons Kapferer, then it must be capable of touching very intense emotions. Like Anderson, Kapferer thus stresses the religious aspect of nationalism and its ability to depict the nation as a sacred community.

In his study of nationalism in Québec, Richard Handler suggests that Québecois nationalists imagine the nation as a 'collective individual'. Citing three different informant statements which support this assumption, he concludes:

These images of the nation as a living individual – a tree, a friend, a creature with a soul – convey first of all a sense of wholeness and boundedness. They establish the integral, irreducible nature of the collectivity as an existent entity. (Handler, 1988: 40)

In general, nationalism, like other ethnic ideologies, appropriates symbols and meanings from cultural contexts which are important in people's everyday experience. During the period leading up to the Islamic Revolution in Iran in 1979, the US was depicted as an adulterous infidel who raped and mistreated Iran, which was depicted as a woman – as a mother-country (Thaiss, 1978). This kind of symbolism can be extremely powerful in mass politics.

This example also confirms the view of nationalism (and other ethnic ideologies) as a form of metaphoric kinship. Kinship terms are frequently used in nationalist discourse (mother-country, father of the nation, brothers and sisters, and so on), and the abstract community postulated by nationalists may be likened to the kin group. Although principles of kinship vary, the members of every society have some notion of family obligations. Kinship and kin organisation are basic features of social organisation in most societies. Nationalism appeared, and continues to appear, in periods when the social importance of kinship is weakened. One may perhaps go so far as to say that urbanisation and individualism create a social and cultural vacuum in human lives in so far as kinship loses much of its importance. Nationalism promises to satisfy some of the same needs that kinship was formerly responsible for. It offers security and a feeling of continuity, as well as offering career opportunities (through the educational system and the labour market). As a metaphorical *pater familias* nationalism states that the members of the nation are a large family: through the national courts it punishes its disobedient children. It is an abstract version of something concrete which every individual has strong emotions about, and nationalism tries to transfer this emotional power to the state level. In this way, nationalism appears as a metaphoric kinship ideology tailored to fit large-scale modern society – it is the ideology of the nation-state.

The nation-state

Like other ideologies, nationalism must simultaneously justify a particular (real or potential) power structure and satisfy acknowledged needs on the part of a population. Seen from this perspective, a successful nationalism implies the linking of an ethnic ideology with a state apparatus. There are important differences between the functioning of such a state and other social systems studied by anthropologists.

The nation-state, unlike many other political systems, draws on an ideology proclaiming that political boundaries should be coterminous with cultural boundaries. Further, the nation-state has a monopoly on the legitimate use of violence and taxation. This double monopoly is its most important source of power. The nation-state has a bureaucratic administration and a written legislation which encompasses all citizens, and it has – at least as an ideal – a uniform educational system and a shared labour market for all its citizens. The great majority of nation-states have a national language used in all official communications; some deny linguistic minorities the right to use their vernacular.

Political leaders in other kinds of society may also monopolise violence and taxation. What is here peculiar to the nation-state is the enormous concentration of power it represents. The difference is apparent between a modern war and a feud among the Yanomamö or Nuer. In the same way as the abstract community of nationalism includes an inconceivable number of people (in Britain about 60 million) compared with polities based on kinship (the upper limit for a Yanomamö local community is approximately 500 individuals), the modern state can be said to be modelled on social organisations based on kinship.

Having discussed general aspects of nationalist identity, ideology and organisation, we shall now consider some examples which suggest ways in which nationalism can be studied anthropologically.

Nationalism against the state

The cultural egalitarianism preached by nationalism in most of its manifestations can inspire counterreactions in situations where a segment of the population does not consider itself to be part of the nation. This is extremely common, as most nation-states contain larger or smaller minorities. In chapter 7, different minority situations will be considered; here, we shall briefly consider one where a part of the minority reacts through inventing its own nation.

The egalitarian charter of French nationalism and the French Revolution emphasised that every citizen should have equal rights, equal juridical rights and, in principle, equal opportunities (women, however, were only partly included in this imagined community). Eventually all French people were to identify themselves as French-people and feel loyal towards the new republic. Linguistic standardisation through the spread of the official French language has been an important aspect of this project since the eighteenth century, but linguistic minorities still exist, notably in the south and

south-east and in Brittany, where the majority of the population traditionally spoke Breton, a Celtic language unrelated to French.

Breton ethnic identity is intimately connected with language; there
are few other conspicuous markers available for boundary maintenance. This identity has been threatened for centuries by the dominant
French language. Particularly during the first half of the twentieth
century, the number of Breton-speakers declined rapidly. However,
as Maryon McDonald (1989) and others have shown, there have been
signs of ethnic revitalisation in later years. A plethora of organisations championing the Breton cause have emerged since the Second
World War. Lois Kuter (1989) reports that young Bretons have a
positive view on learning Breton, explicitly linking it with their ethnic
identity. Some radio and TV programmes are now made in Breton,
and many learn Breton as a foreign language at evening classes and
summer schools. The language, as well as many aspects of imputed
Breton custom, have largely had to be revived, since the 'acculturation' process had gone very far.

Why do the survival and revival of the Breton language seem so
important to many Bretons? It would be simplistic to say, as an explanation, that their language forms an important part of their cultural
identity. After all, language shift has been widespread in Brittany (and
elsewhere) for centuries. The militancy concerning language can
therefore be seen as an anti-French political strategy. Since the French
state chose the French language as the foremost symbol of its nationalism, the most efficient and visible kind of resistance against that
nationalism may be a rejection of that language. For many years it
was illegal to speak Breton in public. Many Bretons are still bilingual
and switch situationally between the languages. By using Breton in
public contexts, Bretons signal that they do not acquiescence in French
domination. A notion of cultural roots alone would not have been
enough: roots were never sufficient to revive a vanishing identity.

An interesting feature of the Breton resistance against French
domination is an aspect of what Eric Hobsbawm (1977) has called 'the
Shetlands effect', whereby a small periphery allies itself with a major
centre against its local dominator. In the case of some Breton leaders,
this effect was articulated in taking a pro-German line during the
Second World War (McDonald, 1989: 123).

The population of Brittany is divided over the issues of language,
identity and political rights (cf. McDonald, 1989). The revitalisation
movement is largely an elite or middle-class phenomenon, like many
other similar movements (cf. chapter 5 for Indo-Trinidadians).
Cost–benefit calculations may be involved here. Had Brittany been

the wealthiest part of France, Bretons might, like some Catalans in Spain, have demanded full independence.

Nationalism and the Other

Like other ethnic identities, national identities are constituted in relation to *others*; the very idea of the nation presupposes that there are other nations, or at least other peoples, who are not members of the nation. Nationalist dichotomisation may take many forms; it could well be argued that the main structural condition for chauvinist nationalism in our day and age is competition between nation-states on the world market. Although there have been many wars between nation-states, such wars have been comparatively rare since 1945. Instead, we may perhaps regard international sports as the most important form of metaphoric war between nation-states – containing, perhaps, most of the identity-building features of warfare and few of the violent, destructive ones (cf. Archetti, 1991). Nonetheless, boundary maintenance and ethnic dichotomisation may still take violent forms in many parts of the world, and this also holds good for a number of ethnic nationalisms, for example in Sri Lanka.

In his analysis of Sinhalese national symbolism, Kapferer (1988) links state power, nationalist ideology and the Sinhalese–Tamil conflict with the role of Sinhalese myth in cosmology and in everyday life. Important myths, recorded in the ancient Sinhalese chronicle of the *Mahavamsa*, are the Vijaya and Dutugemunu legends. The Vijaya myth, the main Sinhalese myth of origin, tells of a prince who arrives from India and slaughters a great number of demons in order to conquer Sri Lanka. The Dutugemunu myth, set at a later historical period, tells of a Sinhalese leader under whose military guidance the people rids itself of a foreign overlord. Later, he conquers the Tamils.

In Sinhalese political discourse, these myths are frequently 'treated as historical fact or as having foundation in fact' (Kapferer, 1988: 35). Sinhalese dominance in the Sri Lankan state, including dominance over the Tamil minority, is justified by referring to the *Mahavamsa*, which is so interpreted as to state that the Sinhalese and the Tamils have the same origins, but are now two nations, with the Sinhalese as the dominant one. The myths thus form an important element in the justification of Sinhalese nationalism. Tamils produce contradictory interpretations of the myths, which are thus actively used in reconstruction of the past aimed at justifying present political projects.

Kapferer is particularly concerned with violence and the interpenetration of lived experience, myth and state power. When he analyses the ethnic riots of the early 1980s, he finds that 'the demonic

passions of the rioting were fuelled in a Sinhalese Buddhist nationalism that involved cosmological arguments similar to those in
exorcism, particularly in the rites of sorcery' (Kapferer, 1988: 29).
The human–demon dualism and other – frequently violent – aspects
of myth were transferred to a nationalist ideology justifying Sinhalese
hegemony and violence against Tamils.

According to many nationalist myths, the nation is born, or arises,
from a painful rite of passage where it has to fight its adversaries; the
Other or the enemy within. Re-enactment of that violence, as in Sri
Lanka, can be justified by referring to such myths, which form part
of a 'cosmic logic' or ontology through which the Sinhalese experience
the world (Kapferer, 1988: 79). This cosmic logic, where evil plays an
important part, is congruent with the current ethnic hostilities and
serves as a rationalisation for the use of force.

Kapferer's argument is complex and cannot be reproduced in full
here. It may not be correct that violence is a more or less universal
feature of nationalist imagery, but his analysis is consistent with the
perspective on ethnicity and nationalism developed in this book. He
shows the importance of the Other in the formation of ethnic identity
and illuminates the mediating role of symbols in ethnic ideologies.
They must simultaneously justify a power structure *and* give profound
meaning to people's experience in order to motivate them to give
personal sacrifices for the nation. Finally, Kapferer shows how the
potential power of ethnic identifications is increased manifold when
an ethnic identity is linked with a modern state – when ethnicity
becomes nationalism. My descriptions of nationalism as a metaphoric
kinship ideology and (from peaceful Québec) the depiction of the
nation as a human organism, are perhaps too weak in this context.
In relation to Sinhalese nationalism, appropriate metaphors may
rather be war, birth and death. However, both the peaceful Québecois
nationalism and the violent Sinhalese one share certain features: both
refer to the past and to assumptions of shared culture in imagining
their abstract communities. In other regards, of course, they may not
be comparable, since the Québecois are separatist and the Sinhalese
are not. In Kapferer's words:

The organizing and integrating potential of ideology, the propensity of
certain ideological formations to unify, to embrace persons of varying and
perhaps opposed political and social interests, and to engage them in concerted,
directed action, may owe much to the logic of an ontology that the ideology
inscribes ... Ideology can engage a person in a fundamental and what may
be experienced as a 'primordial' way. And so the passions are fired and
people may burn. (Kapferer, 1988: 83)

Kapferer's analysis of Sri Lankan nationalism focuses on the enactment of boundary mechanisms at different interrelated levels; symbolic, practical and political. He argues that nationalisms must be studied in a truly comparative spirit, and shows that Sinhalese nationalism is qualitatively different from European nationalisms because the societies differ. Notably, he argues that it is hierarchical in nature and not inherently egalitarian. Nevertheless, Kapferer's study is consistent with the theoretical framework on ethnic organisation and identity developed in earlier chapters, as well as the theory of nationalism which stresses the link between ethnicity and the state.

The problem of identity boundaries

Problems of identity and problems of boundary maintenance have usually been studied in relation to minorities or otherwise 'threatened' or 'weak' groups, or in situations of rapid social change. It seems to have been an implicit assumption that identity processes and the maintenance of identity are unproblematic in dominant groups. 'Majority identities', Diana Forsythe writes (1989: 137), '... appear as they are seen from without, seeming ... to be strong and secure, if not outright aggressive. Certainly this is how Germanness is perceived in many parts of Europe.'

Forsythe's research on German identity indicates that this central and powerful identity – considered by many as *the* dominant national identity in Europe[3] – is characterised by anomalies, fuzzy boundaries and ambiguous criteria for belongingness. First of all, it is unclear *where* Germany is. Although both the inhabitants of the Federal Republic and the GDR are clearly German (Forsythe's article was written before the reunification), they fail to unite the nation in a nation-state. Not all West Germans would include the GDR as *Inland*. Even after reunification, the distinction between *Wessies* and *Ossies* is a salient one, which refers to economic as well as to imputed cultural differences. Further, many Germans would include the areas lost to Poland and the former USSR during the Second World War as German.

Second, it is difficult to justify the existence of the German nation by referring to history. With the Nazi period (1933–45) in mind, Forsythe writes (1989: 138): 'The German past is not one that lends itself comfortably to nostalgia, nor is it well-suited to serve as a charter for nationalists' dreams for the future.'

Third, more or less as a consequence, it is difficult to state what it means to be German in cultural terms. Pride in national identity has

---

3 This is perhaps particularly true after reunification in 1990.

positively been discouraged since the Second World War, as many 'typical' aspects of German culture were associated with Nazism (cf. Dumont, 1992, for a cultural–historical analysis of German national identity).

Fourth, and this is the issue which is of particular concern here, the question of *who is German* turns out to be a complicated one. In principle, 'the universe is divided into the theoretically exhaustive and mutually exclusive categories of *Deutsche* (Germans) and *Ausländer* (foreigners)' (Forsythe, 1989: 143). In practice, there are nevertheless difficult problems associated with the delineation of boundaries. The criterion for Germanness can be either language or 'a mixture compounded of appearance, family background, country of residence, and country of origin' (ibid.). A certain number of foreigners are included in both definitions of Germanness, and the latter especially is quite inaccurate. Austrians and the majority of Swiss are German-speakers, but do not live in a German state. On the other hand, millions of people of German descent, who may or may not actually speak German, live in Central and Eastern Europe.[4] These, as well as other emigrants, fall into different categories (see Figure 6.1).

The category *Ausländer* (foreign) presents similar problems, and it transpires that the Dutch and Scandinavians are considered much 'less foreign' than Turks and Jews.

These anomalies, while they pose specific problems to German identity, are general and widespread. Such problems highlight the lack of congruence between ideal models or ideologies and that social reality to which they ostensibly refer. Nationalist and other ethnic ideologies hold that social and cultural boundaries should be unambiguous, clear-cut and 'digital' or binary. They should also be congruous with spatial, political boundaries. This, as we have seen, is an ideal which is very difficult to uphold in practice. Some violent nationalisms may try to eradicate the anomalies; such was the case of Nazism, where millions of members of so-called lower races occupying parts of German territory were killed or forced to emigrate. In most cases, however, complex realities are coped with more gracefully. We should here keep in mind that there is never a perfect fit between an ideology and the social reality it is about, since an ideology is a kind of theory – like a map – which necessarily simplifies the concrete.

---

4 The foreign policy spokesman for the German Social Democratic Party stated, at a public lecture in 1992, that 'there are six million Germans living in the former Soviet Union.'

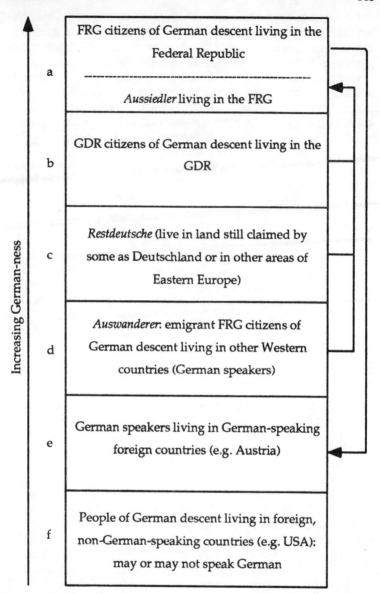

Figure 6.1: Degrees of German-ness according to emic categories
Source: Forsythe, 1989: 146.

German identity, although ideally solid, digital and well demarcated, actually functions in an *analogic* way: differences of degree are made relevant in the classification of others even when the classificatory system in theory requires clear dichotomisation. It is possible to be 'somewhat German' or 'not really foreign'. Perhaps nationalist ideologies tend to be more concerned with clear-cut, unambiguous boundaries than other ethnic ideologies. An explanation for this could be that nations are territorial and political units with an inherent need to divide others into insiders and outsiders on the basis of citizenship. Cultural similarity among citizens becomes a political programme vested in the state. In this way, national identities may, generally speaking, be more comprehensive and may place greater demands on the individual than ethnic identities in a polyethnic society.

As the above examples indicate, although it may be correct to talk of *a* general theory of nationalism, namely that presented in the first pages of this chapter, nationalisms on the ground are quite different. So far, all of the nationalisms considered have been clearly ethnic in character. Sinhalese nationalism acknowledges the presence of Sri Lankan Tamils as a distinctive ethnic group, but places them in a subservient relationship to the Sinhalese. We shall therefore round off this chapter by considering the possibility of a nationalism which is *not* based on ethnicity.

A non-ethnic nationalism?

So-called plural or polyethnic societies have often been described as deeply divided societies marked by perennial conflict and competition between discrete ethnic groups (M.G. Smith, 1965; Horowitz, 1985). Although this view may in some cases be relevant, we have argued against it for too strongly focusing on conflict and group boundaries, at the cost of underestimating cooperation, identity formation along non-ethnic lines, and cultural integration. Mauritius is often regarded as a typical plural society (Benedict, 1965); here, I shall approach it from a different perspective, focusing on shared meaning rather than group competition.

There are two complementary trends in Mauritian nationalism, and both of them are ostensibly non-ethnic in character (Eriksen, 1988; 1992a). First, the Mauritian nation may be depicted as identical with the 'mosaic of cultures' reified in the identity politics of the island. Typical expressions of this view of the nation are the cultural shows organised annually in connection with Independence Day (Republic Day as from 1992). At these shows, every main ethnic category is invited to present a 'typical' song or dance from its cultural repertoire. The Sino-Mauritians are always present with a dragon of some kind, Hindus sing Indian film songs or play sitar music, and the Creoles are always represented with a *séga* (a song form associated with the Creoles). In this way, the nation is imagined as a mosaic. This trend, which we may label 'multiculturalism', is also evident in the national mass media, where every group is represented through specific radio and TV programmes, and in the educational system, where pupils may learn their 'ancestral languages' as a foreign language.

The other main trend in Mauritian nationalism depicts the nation as a supra-ethnic or non-ethnic community, which encompasses or transcends ethnicity rather than endorsing it. The flag, the national anthem and the national language express such a nationalism. The national language of Mauritius is English, which is no one ethnic group's ancestral language or currently spoken language – and which therefore seems an appropriate choice as a supra-ethnic compromise (Eriksen, 1990). Colonial symbols, which cannot be associated with a particular ethnic group, are also dominant. Formal equality and equal opportunities are emphasised.

The Mauritian situation is more complex than this outline suggests. There is some ethnic tension, and there are conflicts between nationalism and ethnicity. Many post-colonial states are faced with similar problems to those of Mauritius. They are obviously constructions of recent origins. When Immanuel Wallerstein asks, rhetorically, 'Does India exist?' (Wallerstein, 1991a), he must therefore answer no – or at least, that it did not exist prior to colonisation. Many such states, particularly in Africa, had no pre-colonial state that could be revived, and the great majority of these states are polyethnic . To turn nation-building into an ethnic project would in many of these cases lead to unrest, secessionism or civil war. To depict the nation as identical with a 'mosaic of ethnic groups' could, on the other hand, threaten to undermine the project of nation-building since it focuses on differences instead of similarities.

Let us now see how some of the insights developed earlier may shed light on the Mauritian situation. From the study of ethnic processes on the interpersonal level – from the early Copperbelt studies onwards – we know that identities are negotiable and situational. From the Barthian emphasis on boundary processes and later studies of identity boundaries, we also know that the selection of boundary markers is arbitrary in the sense that only some features of culture are singled out and defined as crucial in boundary processes. Just as the potential number of nations is much larger than the actual number, the number of ethnic groups in the world is potentially infinite. From recent studies of nationalism, finally, we have learnt that the relationship between cultural practices and reified culture is not a simple one, and that ideologists always select and reinterpret aspects of culture and history which fit into the legitimation of a particular power constellation.

On the basis of these theoretical insights, it is possible to draw the conclusion that Mauritian nationalism may represent an attempt to create a nation in the conventional sense; that Mauritian society is currently at an early stage of the ethnogenesis of a nation. The invention of a shared history for all the ethnic groups of the island is under way, and a plausible 'myth of origin' for the nation could be the last ethnic riot, in 1967–8, the 'riot to end all riots'. The homogenisation of cultural practices has gone very far, due to rapid industrialisation and capitalist integration, and by 1993 the vast majority of Mauritians spoke the same language at home (*Kreol*, a French-lexicon creole). As an increasing part of the individual's life is determined by his or her performance in the anonymous labour market, the supra-ethnic variety of national identity may eventually replace obsolete ethnic identities.

On the other hand, a principal lesson from ethnicity studies is that doomed ethnic categories tend to re-emerge, often with unprecedented force. Referring to 'primordial' values, they remain capable of mobilising people – years after the social contexts where these values were enacted had vanished. Mauritius may remain a prosperous, stable and democratic society based on a plurality of ethnic identities which are compatible with national identity – and this is also a possible outcome of the current process of transformation.

Nationalism and ethnicity reconsidered

Nationalism and ethnicity are kindred concepts, and the majority of nationalisms are ethnic in characer. The distinction between nationalism and ethnicity as analytical concepts is a simple one, if we stick to the formal level of definitions. A nationalist ideology is an ethnic ideology which demands a state on behalf of the ethnic group. However, in practice the distinction can be highly problematic.

First, nationalism may sometimes express a polyethnic or supraethnic ideology which stresses shared civil rights rather than shared cultural roots. That would be the case in many African countries as well as in Mauritius, where no ethnic group openly tries to turn nation-building into an ethnic project on its own behalf. A distinction between ethnic nationalisms and polyethnic or supra-ethnic nationalisms could be relevant here.

Second, certain categories of people may find themselves in a grey zone between nation and ethnic category. If some of their members want full political independence, others limit their demands to linguistic and other rights within an existing state. It depends on the interlocutor whether the category is a nation or an ethnic group. Moreover, national and ethnic membership can change situationally. A Mexican in the United States belongs to an ethnic group, but belongs to a nation when he or she returns to Mexico. Such designations are not politically innocent. Whereas the proponents of an independent Punjabi state (Khalistan) describe themselves as a nation, the Indian government sees them as ethnic rebels.

Third, in the mass media and in casual conversation the terms are not used consistently. When, regarding the former Soviet Union, one spoke of the '104 nations' comprising the union, this term referred to ethnic groups. Only a handful of them were nations to the extent that their leaders wanted full independence.

In societies where nationalism above all is presented as an impartial and universalistic ideology based on bureaucratic principles of justice, ethnicity and ethnic organisation may appear as threats against national cohesion, justice and the state. This tension may appear as a conflict between *particularist* and *universalist* moralities. In these polyethnic societies, nationalism is frequently presented as a supra-ethnic ideology guaranteeing formal justice and equal rights for everybody. Typically, nationalist rhetoric stressing equality for all belongs to the political left in these societies, such as in Mauritius and South Africa.

A different kind of conflict between ethnicity and nationalism, which is perhaps more true to the conventional meaning of the term nationalism, can be described as a conflict between a dominating and a dominated ethnic group within the framework of a modern nation-state. In such contexts, the nationalist ideology of the hegemonic group will be perceived as a particularist ideology rather than a universalist one, where the mechanisms of exclusion and ethnic discrimination are more obvious than the mechanisms of inclusion and formal justice. This kind of duality, or ambiguity, is fundamental to nationalist ideology (Eriksen, 1991b).

This duality of nationalism has been described as 'the Janus face of nationalism' (Nairn, 1977: part 3). A conflict between ethnicity and nationalism is evident, for example, in the case of the relationship between the Bretons and the French state. This kind of situation is characteristic of the contemporary world, where states tend to be dominated politically by one of the constituent ethnic groups (cf. Connor, 1978) or, more accurately, by its elites. In the next chapter I shall distinguish between two types of minority situation, that of aboriginal or indigenous populations and that of urban minorities, and differences and similarities between their respective situations will be accounted for.

7 MINORITIES AND THE STATE

[F]or their part, the Indians have little or nothing to put in the place of governmental administration: there are no 'typically Indian' methods of administering a hospital nor is there a 'typically Indian' way of bookkeeping or using typewriters.

Eugeen E. Roosens (1989: 72)

Modernisation and the establishment of a system of nation-states have created a new situation for the people nowadays known as 'ethnic minorities' or 'indigenous peoples'. Most of them have become 'citizens', whether they like it or not. The spread of capitalism has also played an important part in creating conditions for new forms of ethnicity – both through local economic and cultural change and through migration. The perspective on ethnicity and nationalism in this chapter can be described as a perspective from below, in that we focus on ethnic groups which are not hegemonic in a state. They remain distinctive despite the efforts undertaken by the agencies of the nation-state to integrate them politically, culturally and economically.

Minorities and majorities

An ethnic minority can be defined as a group which is numerically inferior to the rest of the population in a society, which is politically non-dominant and which is being reproduced as an ethnic category (cf. Minority Rights Group, 1990: xiv).

Like other concepts used in the analysis of ethnicity, the twin concepts minority and majority are *relative* and *relational*. A minority exists only in relation to a majority and vice versa, and their relationship is contingent on the relevant system boundaries. In the contemporary world, these system boundaries are nearly always state boundaries. The majority–minority relationship therefore changes if state boundaries are redrawn. Whereas the Sikhs form a tiny minority in India (1.9 per cent of the total population), they form a majority (slightly over 60 per cent) in Punjab. If the militant Sikh quest for independence eventually is successful, there will still be a 35 per cent Hindu minority in the independent country of Khalistan. In other words, as soon as minorities become majorities due to redefinitions of system boundaries, new minorities tend to appear.

We should also keep in mind that groups which constitute majorities in one area or country may be minorities elsewhere. The Magyars or Hungarians, for example, form a strong majority in Hungary, but large groups of people who consider themselves and are considered by others as Hungarians live in countries (Slovakia, Romania, Serbia and Austria) where they are minorities. Russians, a majority population in the former Soviet Union, have become minorities in many of the post-Soviet nation-states. Immigrant groups can be in a comparable situation; members of these groups belong to a majority (or a nation) in their country of origin, but to a minority (or an 'ethnic group') in the host country. A majority group can also become a minority through the inclusion of its territory in a larger system.

There are possibilities for situational switching, as well as historical change, between minority and majority status for a particular group or category. Here we should note that the group boundaries themselves may well remain more or less unchanged through such a process.

Minorities and the state

In the contemporary world, virtually everybody is forced to take on an identity as a citizen – in the words of David Maybury-Lewis (1984), we are living in Leviathan. Since some forms of cultural and ethnic variation must be 'matter out of place' to nationalists, ethnic variation is frequently defined by dominant groups as a problem, as something one has to 'cope with'. Downright genocide and enforced displacement are the most brutal methods employed by states in their dealings with minorities. Several instances of genocide in the Americas and Australia followed European colonialism; another familiar case was the systematic extermination of German and Central European Jews and Gypsies by the Third Reich before and during the Second World War. Enforced displacement of whole ethnic groups has been carried out by North American colonisers as well as by the Soviet Union under Stalin and by the pre-Columbian Inca kingdom in the Andes, where the Aymara were forcefully displaced. These methods have become less common since the Second World War, notwithstanding violent attempts at 'ethnic cleansing' in former

Yugoslavia. Today, states generally use one or several of three main strategies in their dealings with minorities.

First, the state may insist on the assimilation of 'entropy-resistant elements'. It may insist that, say, minorities such as Bretons and Provençals become French; that they shed their parochial languages and boundary markers and gradually come to identify themselves as French people. Although such policies of assimilation are often believed to help their target groups to achieve equal rights and to improve their social standing, they often inflict suffering and loss of dignity on the part of the minorities, who thus are taught that their own tradition is of no value. In the previous chapter, we saw an example of an ethnic revitalisation movement, the Breton movement, which seemed to compete for no other scarce resource than cultural self-determination. Successful policies of assimilation ultimately lead to the disappearance of the minority. In recent British history, this has been the fate of the Cornish, whose descendants are indistinguishable from the English – that is to say, they *are* English.

Second, the state may opt for domination, which frequently implies segregation on ethnic grounds. This entails the minority being physically removed from the majority, and this is frequently justified by referring to the presumed cultural inferiority of the former. Ideologies of segregation often hold that it is harmful to 'mix cultures' or races, and are concerned with boundary maintenance. The context is always one of power asymmetry although, as we shall see below, it can also be analysed in terms of negotiation. South African apartheid was a very clear case of ethnic segregation, and many North American cities are also segregated along ethnic lines. In the latter case, segregation is not necessarily the result of state policies but is caused by a combination of class differences following ethnic lines, ethnic dichotomisation and minority stigma.

The third main option for the state consists in transcending ethnic nationalist ideology and adopting an ideology of multiculturalism, where citizenship and full civil rights need not imply a particular cultural identity, or a decentralised federal model providing a high degree of local autonomy.

Minorities may respond to state domination in three principal ways; they have the three options described as 'exit, voice or loyalty' by Alfred Hirschmann (1970). The first option is to assimilate. This has been a very common process, whether actually chosen or not. In some cases, it is nevertheless impossible for an ethnic minority to choose assimilation. Blacks in the United States have not been assimilated, largely because skin colour ('race') is an important marker of ethnicity in the US. Skin colour thereby becomes an ethnic characteristic, whether or not blacks themselves emphasise it. In minority–majority relations, therefore, we see the limitations of an analytical perspective on ethnicity which one-sidedly stresses the voluntary, strategic aspect. Many people are indeed *victims* of ethnic classifications which they do not themselves support.

The minorities which are denied assimilation frequently have a subordinate place in the division of labour. They could be considered the victims of ethnic segregation. Other groups, however, actively resist assimilation and react through ethnic incorporation. The second option for minorities thus consists in acquiescing in their subordination, or in other ways trying to coexist peacefully with the nation-state. They may sometimes negotiate for limited autonomy in, say, religious, linguistic or local political matters. In other cases, such groups may reproduce their boundaries and identities informally. Some, such as North American Jews, Sino-Mauritians or Freetown Creoles (in Sierra Leone; cf. A. Cohen, 1981), can even be considered elites.

The third principal option for minorities, exit or secession, is always incompatible with state policies. Groups which favour secession and full independence are always ethnic communities in Handelman's sense, and I have earlier described them as proto-nations.

These strategies are ideal types. In practice, both state tactics and minority responses will usually combine strategies of assimilation and segregation (or ethnic incorporation), and minorities may be divided over issues of independence. A term commonly used to describe combinations between assimilation and segregation/incorporation, is 'integration'. This implies the minority's simultaneous participation in the shared institutions of society *and* its reproduction of group identity and ethnic boundaries. As we shall see below, many majority–minority relationships may be analysed by focusing on the tension between *equality* and *difference* along these lines.

The creation of minorities in the modern world

When did the Yanomamö become a minority? In Chagnon's (1983) classic study, they do not appear as a minority. On the contrary, they were clearly a dominant group divided into clans and lineages, not into ethnic groups. Today the Yanomamö are seen, and their leaders define themselves, as an ethnic minority or an indigenous people. Drawing on international law and on a global network of indigenous peoples, they negotiate with the Venezuelan and the Brazilian governments for territorial rights. Through the dual process of integration into the state and into the capitalist mode of production and system of consumption (cf. chapter 5) the Yanomamö *became* a minority.

Their minority situation is caused by their integration, whether it is willed or not, into a larger system.

When this kind of integration is more or less accomplished, it usually leads to complementary reactions of assimilation and ethnic incorporation. In the case of many minorities, it is possible to trace distinct phases in their strategies. We should note here that the agenda of 'cultural rights' is a recent one in world politics, and that it is only after the Second World War that membership in an ethnic minority can, in some societies, be a political advantage. An important 'ethnicisation' of the world is taking place and, as argued in chapters 4 and 5, this process is linked with modernisation – it is what we could also describe as the politicisation of culture. The Ainu minority of Hokkaido (Japan) was for a long time defined by the dominant Japanese not as an ethnic minority, but as imperfect Japanese (Sjöberg, 1990; cf. Friedman, 1990). Recent ethnic revitalisation among the Ainu, whose leaders stress that 'we have our own culture', has established a new kind of relationship with the Japanese. Instead of being measured by the standards of Japanese society, they now present themselves as *a people*, distinct from and equal to the Japanese; as different rather than inferior. Presented with the choice between being an underclass or an ethnic minority, many groups opt for the latter.

Although this example refers to an indigenous population, the general points made so far are valid for other minorities as well. What they all have in common is a potentially conflictual relationship with the state and/or a dominant group. In the following, I shall distinguish between two main kinds of minority situations: indigenous peoples and urban minorities.

Indigenous peoples

The term 'indigenous people' is used in anthropology to describe a non-dominant group in a delineated territory, with a more or less acknowledged claim to aboriginality (see Paine, 1992, on the term). Aboriginal peoples are not necessarily 'first-comers'. Although the Germans and the Russians may be the oldest extant ethnic groups in parts of their respective territories, they are not considered indigenous peoples. Indigenous groups are defined as non-state people, and they are always linked with a non-industrial mode of production. This does not mean that members of indigenous peoples never take part in governments or work in factories, but rather that they represent a way of life which renders them particularly vulnerable in relation to modernisation and the state. Indigenous peoples have historically been subjected to massive slaughter, forceful assimilation and neglect (Australian aborigines were not even counted in national censuses until the 1960s). In recent years, particularly since the 1970s, many such groups have become politically organised in ways that enable them to promote their interests vis-à-vis the dominant, encompassing majority. The formation of the WCIP (World Council for Indigenous Peoples) has been important in this regard. Seen from the perspective of anthropological theory of ethnicity, the dynamics of such ethnopolitical movements have proved a very fertile ground for the study of identity processes in a situation of change (see, for example, Brass, 1985).

Indigenous peoples stand in a potentially conflictual relationship to the nation-state as an institution. Their main political project is often presented as an attempt to survive as a culture-bearing group, but they rarely or never envision the formation of their own nation-state. They are non-state peoples.

Territorial conflict

The most common kind of conflict between indigenous peoples and the state concerns territorial rights. A typical case of this kind is the continuing dispute between the Cree Indians and the Canadian state over a major hydroelectric project in James Bay. In the 1970s the Canadian authorities decided to build a large dam in the middle of a territory acknowledged to be a traditional hunting ground of the Indians, who protested against what they saw as an illegitimate use of force. The conflict highlighted the difficult political situation of stateless peoples when confronted with a state which formally encompasses their territory. Anthropologists who studied the James Bay dispute nevertheless emphasised the considerable skill displayed by Indian leaders as brokers and negotiators (Feit, 1985). Overall it has been seen as an important event in the formation of Canadian Indian identities (Roosens, 1989): through such confrontations with the state, the Indian groups were effectively organised and succeeded in pooling their political resources, as well as learning how to reify culture and to use it strategically in political negotiations.

A parallel case in northern Scandinavia has been studied by Robert Paine (1985). This case, which was eventually lost by the indigenous people, concerned the building of a hydroelectric dam by the Norwegian government, which it was said would upset the ecology of traditional grazing areas of the transhumant mountain Sami. Paine argues that the Sami depended on mobilising support from the outside – essentially from greater Norwegian society – for their resistance to be of any consequence. The Sami, and other groups in similar situations, are crucially dependent on interethnic *brokers* who can represent their interests in greater society, who can complementarise (Eidheim's term; cf. chapter 2) with the authorities and with world opinion. This kind of political brokerage may increase both the minority's standing in greater society and the self-respect of its members. In the case of the Sami, the resistance against the Alta dam, although ultimately unsuccessful, was instrumental in forging a sense of Sami unity. It laid the organisational foundation for an interesting political experiment, namely the formation in 1989 of a Sami parliament within the Norwegian state. Links were forged within the Sami category, strengthening its network and association aspects (cf. chapter 3), with Norwegian political organisations and non-governmental organisations (NGOs), and with indigenous groups in other parts of the world.

Two general points must be made here. First, there is no necessary contradiction between modernisation and retention of ethnic identity – on the contrary, it can be argued that in many cases certain aspects of modernisation are required for identity maintenance to be successful. It is not cultural change in itself that determines the chances for survival for ethnic minorities. Rather, it is the relative ability of specific minorities to master the changes and utilise new technologies and political possibilities for their own ends (Eidheim, 1992; Henriksen, 1992).

This conclusion coincides well with the perspective on ethnicity developed earlier in this book, which originally grew out of studies of interethnic relations on the Copperbelt, immigrants in the United States, boundary processes in the Sudan and in Swat, and politics in African cities. The fact that it is applicable to such a diversity of contexts ought to indicate that the anthropological perspective on ethnicity has much to recommend it.

The second point is that a minority–majority relationship may involve other agents as well as the two groups. In many conflicts of this kind, third parties may play an important part. Given their inferior military and political power, indigenous people rely to a great extent on international support. The transnational networks of indigenous peoples have been – and are – extremely important in this regard. So is the role of cultural brokers or entrepreneurs: those individuals and agencies which mediate between the indigenous group, the state and international society. Such actors may themselves be formally educated members of the indigenous group, but they may also be foreign anthropologists, missionaries, or NGOs such as Amnesty, Survival International or IWGIA (International Work Group for Indigenous Affairs) (Paine, 1971). In many cases, there may be doubts as to whose interests these brokers actually represent: in Roosens' (1989) and van den Berghe's (1975) view, they may simply be career politicians in search of power. Their role in processes of cultural change can also be a very interesting topic for further investigation.

Stages in ethnogenesis

The process of ethnogenesis which the Greenlandic Inuits have passed through during the last four or five decades brings up a few further points.

For many years before and after the Second World War, the Greenlandic Inuit identity seemed seriously threatened. Greenland was a Danish colony, and a growing number of Inuits, traditionally hunters, were 'acculturated' to a modern way of life. Danish became an increasingly dominant language, notably as a medium of instruction in the schools. The Danes were favourable to the widespread use of Greenlandic, but the Inuits themselves 'wished to make Greenland Danish-speaking in the long run' (Berthelsen, 1990: 335).

As a part of the new trend in international ethnopolitics which gained momentum in the early 1970s, when it became politically legitimate to raise demands on behalf of ethnic minorities, a new group of spokespeople began to question the disappearance of Inuit culture. Since then, and particularly since the introduction of home rule in 1978, Greenlandic has begun to replace Danish in schools, media and officialdom. Other aspects of what is seen as traditional Inuit culture are also being revitalised, such as handicrafts and clothing.

It was only after a long period of cultural change that Inuits began to reflect systematically on their culture and thereby to turn it into a 'thing' which could be reified in books and political statements. Also, people began to assert their identity only when it could no longer be taken for granted.

The form of cultural reflexivity engendered by literacy may be a decisive variable in the ethnic revitalisation of indigenous peoples (Eriksen, 1991c). Since 'culture as a thing' is important in ethnopolitical symbolism, and since it can most effectively be turned into a thing through writing, we can assume that minorities confronted with capitalism and the state stand a better chance of surviving as culture-bearing groups than illiterate groups. Groups which have 'discovered that they have a culture', who have invented and reified their culture, can draw on myths of origin and a wide array of potential boundary-markers that are unavailable to illiterate minorities, which may easily be turned into underclasses. As the Huron example in chapter 4 showed, a glorious and tragic past can actually be acquired.

These reflections lead up to a seeming paradox of ethnopolitics, which may help to clarify the complex relationship between ethnicity and culture that has been discussed in earlier chapters. For the emphasis on literacy and negotiations with the state in ethnic survival seems to imply that in order to save 'a culture' one must first lose it! This assumption is strengthened by the fact that the leaders of a dominated group must master the cultural codes of the dominant group in order to present their case efficiently.

Modernisation may be said to reduce the scope of cultural variation in the world. However, the emerging cultural self-consciousness or reflexivity brought about through these very processes has also inspired the formation of ethnic identities stressing cultural uniqueness. Simplistically, we may put it like this: while one's grandparents may have lived as traditional Inuits (or Sami, or Scots ...) without giving it any thought,[1] and one's parents took great pains to escape from their stigmatised and shameful minority position and to become assimilated and modern, today's generation does everything in its power to revive the customs and traditions that their grandparents followed without knowing it, and which their parents tried so hard to forget (cf. Giddens, 1990, 1991, on reflexivity and modernity). Similar identity processes may result from various forms of sustained culture contact, but they become especially acute and politically important during the rapid social changes brought about through modernisation.

Factors in indigenous ethnogenesis

Potential conflicts between indigenous groups and the nation-state are activated when the majority wishes to control resources – ecological, economic or human – in the territory of the indigenous population. This may partly explain why questions concerning the 'Fourth World' have grown steadily more prominent, as the nation-state and capitalism exert a direct influence on an increasing number of people in the world. The ethnopolitical movements described earlier are attempts to cope with this development. They are not necessarily directed against modernisation, but against what they see as attempts to violate their territorial rights and their rights to define their own way of life.

---

1 The word Inuit means 'human being'. It is not, in other words, an ethnic label, nor does it suggest that its carriers see themselves as members of 'a culture'.

In Botswana, tension between indigenes and the majority has been unfolding with increasing intensity since the early 1980s (Wilmsen, 1989; Gulbrandsen, 1992). The San people (or *basarwa*, as they are called in Tswana) do not constitute an 'ethnic group' or even an ethnic category in the sense that we use the terms. They are socially and politically fragmented. They are a culturally heterogeneous category of hunters and gatherers.[2] The categorisation of the San as an ethnic group is imposed from the outside.

The San have lost large parts of their original territory. By the early 1990s, perhaps only 5 per cent of the San are actually hunter-gatherers. Many are itinerant wageworkers, who nevertheless continue to live in a nomadic way. As a compensation, the authorities of Botswana founded a development scheme in the 1980s which was intended to 'help' San to become sedentary peasants. Villages are founded for them. Schools, post offices and dispensaries are being built, and a few are offered work in local industries. The programme can be regarded as an attempt to assimilate the San.

Attempts to force indigenous groups to become sedentary and literate are typical of the nation-state, and nomadic peoples are almost everywhere in a difficult situation. There are two chief reasons for this. First, all territories *belong* to someone, either individuals, companies or the state in a modern country. Second, the administration and surveillance of itinerant minorities present great problems. Property rights, the judicial system, the taxation system and the notion of equal rights and duties for everybody are aspects of the modern state which are incompatible with the traditional way of life of many indigenous peoples.

Drawing on research on indigenous peoples elsewhere, we may suggest two principal possible scenarios for the San. One is their eventual assimilation, possibly as a 'low caste', into Botswana society. The other consists of ethnic revitalisation and active ethnopolitics vis-à-vis the authorities. This alternative requires that they establish a political organisation enabling them to present their demands in an efficient way. This in turn requires that they develop an indigenous elite of interethnic brokers. These two scenarios are not mutually exclusive: each of them may apply for different persons or in different situations.

---

2 The Inuits and the Sami may also, following standard criteria of anthropology, be described as culturally heterogeneous, in spite of their shared ethnic identities. The mode of subsistence, dress code and language vary significantly within the ethnic category.

Indigenous peoples may seem to be trapped between cultural genocide and the reservation. They may try to choose isolation in order to retain their tradition – and this seems impossible. They may also try to pursue their political interests through channels defined by the state – and for this to be possible they must first go through a process of cultural adaptation. My distinction between culture and ethnic identity, and the parallel distinction between tradition and traditionalism, indicate that ethnic incorporation – seemingly paradoxically – can be successful during a process of profound cultural change.

There is a problem of authenticity involved in ethnogenesis, but the job of the anthropologist consists of *studying* it rather than *asking* it. When Roosens declared to fellow academics in Québec that he wished to study the Hurons, many advised him not to, since they were no longer 'real Indians'. His colleagues thus seemed to distinguish between 'real' and 'artificial' culture. Such a distinction cannot be anthropologically valid, since it is itself culturally produced. Criteria for authentic ethnic identity are generated intraethnically as well as interethnically, and the dynamics of these criteria are themselves part of that social reality we study. If a Sami who plays lead guitar in a rock group can present himself credibly vis-à-vis other Sami and vis-à-vis greater society *as a Sami*, then it is a social fact that one can be an authentic Sami *and* play lead guitar.[3]

Urban minorities

Immigrants are in several important respects different from indigenous peoples. They often lack citizenship in the host country, and they were often members of majorities in their country of origin. In many cases, immigrants are only temporarily settled in the host country. Unlike indigenous people, labour migrants tend to be totally integrated in the capitalist system of production, since they usually arrive as prospective wageworkers. By this token, refugees are a slightly different category, and it may often be useful to distinguish them from labour migrants.

This section focuses to a great extent on the situation of non-European migrants to European cities. This does not mean that labour migration and urban minorities are chiefly European phenomena, but many major anthropological studies of urban minorities of this kind

---

3 The example was not arbitrarily chosen: there is a large number of local rock groups in the Sami strongholds of Karasjok and Kautokeino, several of them profoundly influenced by the likes of Frank Zappa, sometimes with Sami lyrics.

have been carried out in Europe and the Middle East. Towards the end of this section, we shall consider the minority situation in the United States. At the outset, we should note that this kind of minority research is strongly ideologically charged – and this holds true on both sides of the Atlantic – because the studies usually deal with conflicts in the author's own society, and can thus often be interpreted as (even if they were not intended as) political statements.

As described in chapter 5, changes in the labour markets have been instrumental in the creation of permanent urban minorities in Europe and North America (and elsewhere in the world). Like the minority situations of 'Fourth World' populations, their relationships with dominant groups have to a great extent been studied – particularly by sociologists – as relationships marked by unequal power and economic, political and cultural domination. Studies inspired by Marxist thought have argued that ethnic discrimination in industrial societies is contingent on the class relations in those societies. Immigrant groups, which tend to occupy a low-ranking position in the division of labour, have thus been seen as a reserve labour force which was imported when there was a demand for labour, and which is neglected and sometimes expelled during recessions. Conflicts between immigrants and domestic working classes, sometimes taking the shape of racism and rioting, have sometimes been regarded within this framework as being 'functional' for the system as a whole, since they divert attention from the fundamental contradiction between labour and capital.

Urban minority studies focusing on the level of interpersonal relationships and group dynamics have usually considered the power asymmetry between minority and majority as an important context. We may initially distinguish four aspects of these minority situations which have received much attention:

(i)   Discrimination and disqualification from the dominant population (Cox, 1976; Rex, 1973; Patterson, 1977). Disqualification means that the migrant's skills are unrecognised in the host country. If, for example, she speaks four African languages, that is usually not an asset in the British labour market.

(ii) Minority strategies for the maintenance of group identity (Novak, 1971; Glazer and Moynihan, 1963; Tajfel, 1978; Epstein, 1978; Leman, 1987).

(iii) Group competition and ethnic conflict (Banton, 1983; A. Cohen, 1974a; Despres, 1975b).

(iv) Cultural change in migrant groups (De Vos and Romanucci-Ross, 1975; Leman, 1987).

A fifth interesting field for research, which has so far not been granted proportionate attention, concerns the relationship between the country or village of origin and the host country in the lives of migrants. Many move back and forth, and there are many families which cannot be said to be permanently settled in either location.

It should be noted that immigrant groups may well occupy elite positions in societies. This has obviously been the case, for example, with British settlers in Kenya and a fair proportion of Jews in the United States.

I shall now exemplify how anthropological perspectives on ethnicity may shed light on the kind of minority situation characteristic of urban labour migrants in Europe.

Boundary processes

In a comparison between two polyethnic areas in London, Sandra Wallman (1986) found interesting differences in majority–minority relationships. Bow in the East End (in Tower Hamlets) was marked by strong polarisation and dichotomisation between the traditional residents and immigrants, whereas ethnic relations in Battersea (south London) were much more relaxed and socially less important. Both areas could be described as working-class, and there are approximately as many immigrants from the same places (India, Pakistan, Africa, the West Indies) in both areas. How can we account for the differences?

The social networks in the two areas were differently constituted, and ethnic boundary mechanisms functioned differently. In Bow, the social networks tended to be dense and closed; people interacted with the same partners in many different contexts. In Battersea, on the contrary, people belonged to many different groups with only partly overlapping membership. In Bow, people lived and worked in the same area; people who lived in Battersea worked in other parts of London. In Bow, people characteristically worked at one of a few major factories, whereas those who lived in Battersea had a greater choice and were employed in a greater variety of smaller and larger enterprises. Bow was an area with an old, stable English population, whereas the population of Battersea was more transient. In Bow, housing was largely municipal and did not allow for the same choice as in Battersea, which offered a variety of different kinds of housing. In Bow, only old English (or Irish) families were considered full members of the local community; in Battersea, one 'belonged' the moment one moved in. Wallman describes the difference between the areas as that between a closed homogeneous system (Bow) and an open heterogeneous system (Battersea). The result was that the ethnic boundaries in Bow were much more solid than in Battersea, where ethnicity proved less important (see Figure 7.1). There were several 'gates', or independent points of entry, into the various social subsystems of Battersea, whereas in Bow one would have to pass all the 'hurdles' at once in order to be accepted:

When all your resources are in one overlapping local system, the possibilities for adaptation are much more limited, and your social relationships tend to be multiplex, – i.e. the person you work with is also your neighbour etc. – local relations are not linked with domains or systems outside in the same way, and ethnic groups are more likely to remain distinct. (Wallman, 1986: 243)

The model suggested by Wallman, while describing relationships in a polyethnic city, may fruitfully be applied to other contexts of ethnicity. Her main point is that the salience of ethnicity varies and that this variation can be investigated by looking at *who does what with whom and for which purposes*. If ethnic networks are relevant in some domains, such as the job market, the likelihood for the development of ethnic associations increases. Surely, one may argue that the underlying causes for a particular configuration are structural. One may, for instance, show how the very presence of migrants, and the very competition for housing and jobs, is caused by the capitalist system. Such analyses may be valuable in their own right, but they really omit too many issues if the purpose is to investigate the importance of ethnicity *in people's lives*.

Does culture matter among urban migrants?

In an influential study of Pakistanis in London, John Rex and Robert Moore (1967) argued that Pakistanis were 'turned into a lower class' because of systematic discrimination in the labour and housing markets. Badr Dahya (1974) has argued against this analysis, showing how the 'low' Pakistani standard of living was in fact consistent with their own economic priorities. The Pakistanis themselves, according to Dahya, regarded the British emphasis on 'good housing' as wasteful and as an irrational investment of assets. This difference in evaluation indicates a systematic difference of values between the two groups. Those social workers, politicians and researchers who defined the Pakistani areas as 'slums' and blamed the British authorities or the class system for the poor housing condition of the immigrants could thus be criticised for an ethnocentric view and for not taking the migrants' own evaluations of their situation sufficiently into account.

In a similar vein, Harald Tambs-Lyche (1980) has demonstrated how the religion and caste system of Gujerati Patidars could influence their

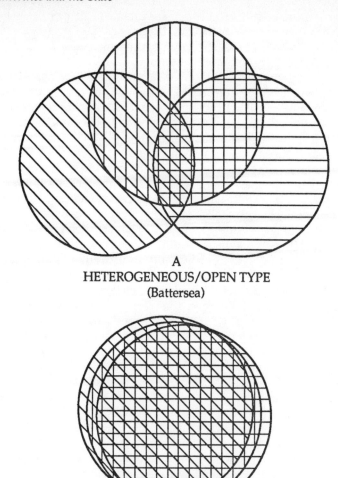

A
HETEROGENEOUS/OPEN TYPE
(Battersea)

B
HOMOGENEOUS/CLOSED TYPE
(Bow)

Figure 7.1: Local systems in Battersea and Bow showing boundary overlap, density and reach of local connections

Source: Wallman, 1986: 241.

adaptation to the British economic system. Their priorities were evidently different from those of the majority, as was their social organisation, and these resources provided them with a comparative advantage in petty commodity trading.

In general, the role of cultural differences in ethnic relations has not been sufficiently studied. Whereas there is a mass of studies available which deal with power inequalities, the social reproduction of group boundaries, group competition and political identities, the 'cultural stuff' that the boundaries contain – to use Barth's formulation – has not been granted proportionate attention. We may therefore state, slightly simplistically, that anthropological and sociological ethnicity studies have dealt with political processes and identity processes, but not really with cultural processes. Cultural differences are analytically elusive – they cannot be measured. An important point for anthropologists writing on ethnicity has also been precisely that there is no one-to-one relationship between cultural variation and ethnicity – indeed, as I have repeatedly argued, ethnic differentiation may partly be an effect of cultural homogenisation. Besides, there are certain political and moral dangers associated with an analytical emphasis on cultural differences between groups. Such an emphasis may both contribute to an untenable reification of culture and contribute to reproducing native ideology and native stereotypes. Partly for these reasons, anthropologists writing on ethnic relations have tended not to stress cultural differences, focusing instead on social processes (cf. Bentley, 1987; Eriksen, 1991b; Haaland, 1992).

On the other hand, it is well known that the evaluations and priorities of different ethnic groups may differ. In many cases, notions of 'the good life' differ systematically between ethnic groups. Such differences, which are often recognised by the actors themselves, may form an important basis for the production of stereotypes and boundary maintenance. The Gypsy–*Gorgio* (Gypsy term for non-Gypsy) dichotomisation in contemporary European societies, for example, rests on perceptions of mutual cultural differences and value differences, the effects of which may be observed in actual social processes (Okely, 1983; Stewart, 1991). People who define themselves as Gypsies clearly have different aspirations and pursue different goals from those of the majority population. When they stereotype the *Gorgios* as unclean and dishonourable people, they generalise from their interpretations of observed *Gorgio* behaviour. Thus, ethnic relations cannot always be fully understood by way of analyses of competition or domination, but may also be regarded as 'encounters between cultures'. The goals people try to achieve are contextually or culturally defined, and in complex multi-ethnic societies members of different groups may pursue different goals.

In a study of West Indian immigrants in Bristol, Ken Pryce (1979) develops this idea further by showing how different groups of West Indians pursue very different life-projects. Two basic value-orientations are prevalent among his informants. One orientation can be labelled 'expressive–disreputable' and is cultivated by 'hustlers', Rastafarians and other groups who reject the mainstream 'respectable' British lifestyle and have a more flexible and fluid adaptation to the educational system and to the labour and housing markets. The other main orientation, which is labelled 'stable law-abiding', is prevalent among regular wageworkers and members of the small West Indian middle class. It is difficult to say to what extent these respective moralities are chosen or imposed by structural conditions. What matters here, however, is the fact that they seem highly congruent with the dual moral systems of 'respectability' and 'reputation' found in the Caribbean itself (P. Wilson, 1978). As in the case of the Patidars, cultural resources have been moved from one context and adapted to a new one. The outcome is a polyethnic British social system which also displays systematic cultural variations.

In modern societies where uniformity and cultural 'likeness' are either encouraged or implicitly taken for granted by the state, it is important to investigate such cultural aspects of ethnicity. In relation to official policies, this question concerns the difficult relationship between equality and difference. On the one hand, every individual is entitled to the same rights; on the other hand, ethnic minorities may be entitled to retain their identity. This potential problem, which I have already discussed in relation to indigenous peoples and the state, is also pertinent with regard to the place of immigrant minorities in greater society. Apart from shedding light on cultural dynamics and identity processes, anthropological research into these issues may provide essential insights for policy-makers.

Identities and 'cultures'

It is commonly held that second- and third-generation immigrants in European cities experience identity problems because they 'live in two cultures' (Liebkind, 1989; Leman, 1987; cf. chapter 4). In talking about immigrants here, we generally mean non-European immigrants, although, for example, Finns in Sweden and South Europeans in other countries are locally categorised as immigrants 'with a distinctive culture and their own values'. Generally, only those immigrants who are locally perceived as significantly culturally distinctive are regarded as immigrants. Diana Forsythe (1989) thus reports that some Germans protested when she classified herself as a 'foreigner', presumably because she was white and spoke German well. Similarly, a Swedish–Danish marriage is not perceived as a mixed marriage in the same way as a Croatian–Danish marriage is.

Research on identity processes and perceptions of self among second- or third-generation immigrants generally tends to confirm that (i) a clear 'acculturation' in terms of values and general orientation has taken place; (ii) the people in question may switch situationally between a largely (say) 'Swedish' and a 'Turkish' identity; (iii) there is often tension between these individuals and their parents; and (iv) the boundaries preventing full assimilation may be both internally and externally constructed (in the latter case, discrimination may prevent full assimilation). There is no clear evidence for the assumption that it is inherently problematic to 'live in two cultures', but such ambiguous situations can certainly be difficult to handle in an environment where one is expected to have a clear, delineated identity. Second- or third-generation immigrants thus become anomalies, not primarily by virtue of their culture but rather because they fail to fit into the dominant categories of social classification in society.

The children (or children's children) of immigrants, while rarely fully assimilated, generally identify themselves more strongly with the values of the majority than their parents did. In some cases this kind of change may inspire revitalisation movements (see Kelly, 1989, on Muslims in Britain), but it may also lead to a diminution in the social importance of ethnicity. In societies where ethnicity is relatively important, the former option seems the more likely. Such ethnic organisations can of course be seen as expressions of identity and/or as political strategies (which is a common perspective), but they may equally well be regarded as defensive responses against discrimination and the refusal of the majority to allow them to assimilate. In these situations, as in other interethnic situations, both parties involved will attempt to define the terms for interaction, and may invoke aspects of cultural equality and difference situationally when it serves their interests.

As noted above (cf. also chapter 5), studies of contact between immigrants and host populations have indicated that cultural differentiae are not entirely irrelevant to ethnicity, although anthropologists have gone a long way in relativising their importance by stressing that it is only when *cultural differences make a social difference* that they contribute to the creation of ethnicity. However, it is clear that whereas language, for example, can be analysed as an ethnic boundary marker, it is also an important aspect of cultural competence in its own right and not an arbitrary ethnic symbol. For second- or third-generation immigrants in Britain, their mastery of English cultural codes necessarily gives them other options in their identity management than were available to their grandparents. The point is not, therefore, that culture and 'real cultural differences' are unimportant, but that it is the uses to which they are put – by both groups in a contact situation – that give them social relevance. The cultural content of identities changes, as does the *social relevance of cultural content*. The cultural resources that a particular immigrant group brings with it are transformed through contact and 'acculturation', but they are also put to new uses in the new context and thereby their social significance is changed. The grandchild of a Turkish immigrant in Cologne may well be Turkish, but being Turkish in Germany means something different from being Turkish in Turkey.

Ethnicity in the US: race, class and language

The US is in important ways different from European countries. It has no semi-mythical history as a nation; it has been populated through successive migrations from four continents – Europe, Africa, Asia and South America – up to the present. The 1980 census revealed that of the 226.5 million people counted, almost 23 million reported that they spoke another language than English at home. Almost half were speakers of Spanish (Wardhaugh, 1987: 248). This clearly indicates that the US is not an ethnic nation in the same sense as France or Germany is. In addition, millions of Anglophone Americans have non-American 'ethnic identities', such as German, Swedish or Jewish. This form of ethnicity is sometimes spoken of as secondary ethnicity (Nash, 1988), since the people in question would probably primarily regard themselves as Americans.

The American 'ethnic revival' of the 1960s and 1970s received much scholarly attention. Many scholars argued that the 'American melting-pot', which was expected to fuse diverse populations into one (cf. chapter 2), never took place and that American society remained ethnically heterogeneous (Fishman *et al.*, 1966; Glazer and Moynihan, 1963; Novak, 1971). Focusing on 'European' ethnicities, these studies emphasised the dual role of ethnicity in securing political power and in strengthening personal identity.

A look at some of the different ethnic categories and groups in the United States reveals important variations, and shows that it would be oversimplifying to ask bluntly whether or not the 'melting-pot' occurred. One has to be more specific about one's contentions.

American Indians and blacks seem to be 'unmeltable' ethnic categories. They are phenotypically different from the majority and, in the case of many Indian groups, they still insist on their right not to take full part in the labour market and the American political system. Many of them have developed ethnopolitical organisations.

As regards the blacks, their colour can function effectively as an ethnic boundary since cultural stereotypes are associated with dark skin. A major questionnaire survey indicated that 98 per cent of white Americans agreed that blacks are in general worse off than whites (Sniderman and Hagen, 1985). William Wilson (1978) has nevertheless argued that the social significance of 'race' is declining; in other words, that class has become more important than ethnicity in accounting for vertical differentiation in American society. Wilson showed that there had been great upward mobility among blacks, and that the number of poor whites seemed to be on the increase. Wilson's critics have stressed that the rising significance of class origins in determining job opportunities and life-chances in general does not necessarily imply the decreasing significance of ethnicity or 'race' (cf. Willie, 1991). They have stressed the need to analyse the interrelationship between the factors. However, as Comaroff and Comaroff (1992: 67) remark, Wilson's point was that 'the life chances of blacks are determined by other structural factors [than colour]; namely, class differences', even if actors would still *experience* the importance of colour strongly.

With respect to most of the European immigrant groups, the picture is different. There has been widespread intermarriage between them and many millions of Americans could, if they wanted to, trace their origins back to several different European countries. In addition, the possibilities for the preservation of their European heritage were limited for these groups. In order to survive economically, they were forced to adapt to the American labour market and to learn English. Most immigrants lost their vernacular entirely within two generations.

These changes did not in themselves prevent the groups from recodifying their 'culture' and developing ethnic networks and associations. However, as Steinberg (1981) and others have argued, this happened only to a limited degree. The fact that, say, Americans of Scandinavian origin celebrate Scandinavian national days and publish weekly community newspapers does not imply that they are 'Scandinavian' or that ethnicity plays a crucial part in their daily life. Similarly, a New York rabbi interrogated by Epstein (1978) states that American Jews were Jews in the synagogue but 'plain Americans' the rest of the time. One may nevertheless also argue, as Nash (1988) does, that the informal ethnic associations of American Jews go a long way towards explaining their disproportionate success in the social hierarchy. It could also be argued that the divided loyalties of some Americans of non-American origin pose a potential problem. During the Second World War, Americans of Japanese origin were interned because they were suspected of divided loyalties. In other cases, it can be relatively unproblematic to have two or several identities. Among North Americans, there is generally no problem involved in identifying oneself as Ukrainan or Portuguese; the overarching Canadian or US identity is then taken for granted.

In a sense, the melting-pot *did* occur in that diverse immigrant groups acquired the same basic values and the same language, and intermarried to a high degree. At another level, it may *not* have occurred in so far as people still draw resources – symbolic, material or political – from ethnic identifications. Here, the importance of distinguishing between ethnic identity and culture, and between different expressions of ethnicity, is evident. For a member of a Hispanic local community in Spanish Harlem, 'ethnic identity' signifies something quite different from what it means to a Minnesota farmer of Swedish origin.

Native notions of 'race' are crucial for an understanding of American ethnicity. Whereas 'the ethnic revival' was seen as an ideological current based on voluntary identification with (real or imputed) origins, ethnic segregation based on appearance is not voluntary on the part of those who are segregated. Blacks, in particular, and later immigrants from Latin America, have largely been segregated against their own will. In their case, there is also a clear correlation between ethnicity and class membership: they occupy the lower rungs of the class system.

The paradox of multiculturalism

The most recent large immigrant groups to the United States, Catholic Spanish-speakers from Latin America, present an interesting political problem. Unlike earlier immigrant groups, it seems as if they will retain their language for more than two generations – indeed, in some American cities Spanish has become a second official language (amidst strong protests: cf. Wardhaugh, 1987; Fishman, 1989). Spanish-speaking immigrants to the US may in fact prove to be 'unmeltable' in a different way from blacks and Indians. Whereas blacks were to some extent culturally but not ethnically assimilated and Indians partly try to retain their link with a non-industrial mode of production, Spanish-speakers seem to try to retain both their cultural and ethnic identities, yet they are massively urban and pursue typical urban life-projects. If the Spanish-speaking community succeeds in retaining Spanish as a vernacular language, we may witness a new phase in American nation-building, where linguistic uniformity is not seen as a condition for nationhood.

Is this linguistic retention chosen or imposed, and is it an asset or a handicap? Linguistic retention enables a minority to remain distinctive, and simultaneously it prevents the group from achieving equality in a country with another official language. Evidently, this problem is relevant for the discussion of the right of ethnic groups to be distinctive versus the right to be treated as an equal within a state. Both majority and minority will usually have a particular interpretation of this dual principle, and their respective interpretations may be at odds with each other.

The state may be accused of injustice both if it promotes equality *and* if it promotes difference. If the state stresses equal rights and duties, minority members may feel that their cultural distinctiveness is not being respected; that their boundaries and identities are threatened. Minority reactions against French language policies, described in chapter 6, may exemplify this. Similarly, British Gypsies feel that the state is meddling in their affairs when it insists that they should become sedentary wageworkers (Okely, 1983).

If, on the other hand, the dominant group stresses cultural differences and turns them into virtues, minority members may feel that they are being actively discriminated against. This has been the case in South Africa, where black Africans have been denied the same career opportunities as the whites – who have even tried to deny them command of English through encouraging the use of African languages. It also seems to have been the case in Australia, where, in Kapferer's words, aboriginals 'have become so close to the centre of nationalist thought that they have suffered from it' (Kapferer, 1988: 142). They are defined from the outside as 'noble savages' whether they like it or not. In other words, they have not reached true self-determination in the sense of negotiating their identity in their own terms (cf. also Paine, 1992).

The decisive variable here is *power*. Usually the majority has the power to define when minorities should be like themselves and when they should be different. Very often, potential elites are denied the right to be different whereas low classes are denied the right to be equal. In a critique of American ethnicity studies, Stephen Steinberg asserts:

Immigrants [from Europe] were disparaged for their cultural peculiarities, and the implied message was: 'You will become like us whether you want to or not.' When it came to racial minorities, however, the unspoken dictum was, 'No matter how much like us you are, you will remain apart.' (Steinberg, 1981: 42)[4]

This kind of contradiction can sometimes be described as *the paradox of multiculturalism*. In some societies, such as Canada, Mauritius and Australia, ethnic diversity is positively encouraged (up to a point where it can interfere with the state's interests). As a consequence, the citizens are not only given the right to 'have a culture', but in many cases they are positively forced to adorn themselves with an ethnic label, whether they want to or not. Sometimes groups are given differential treatment on the basis of presumed cultural distinctiveness – and thus some of their members may complain that they are deprived of equal treatment.

Public controversies over culture

Ethnic minorities are no more homogeneous than other categories of people, and there may be important differences in views and values within minorities. In Mauritius, it transpired during the 1980s that the Muslim 'community' was seriously divided over an issue of differential treatment. Up to 1987, the Muslims had been allowed to settle domestic court matters according to Muslim law even when it was at odds with Mauritian law. When the law was removed, it became evident that many Muslims, most of them women, had for years been against that law. A similar issue came up in Norway in 1990–1, and it concerned the country's tiny Gypsy minority. For years, Norwegian authorities had informally allowed Gypsy parents to take their children out of school at an early age 'because the *Gorgio* school was in conflict with their culture'. Not unexpectedly, a young Gypsy accused the state of being responsible for his illiteracy.

Public debates similar to these are common in many European countries. In France, a major issue in the late 1980s concerned the right of Muslim girls at school to wear a headscarf signifying religious adherence. French schools are non-confessional. In Britain, an important public issue has concerned the limits of tolerance vis-à-vis Muslim fundamentalists, particularly in connection with the Rushdie case. In several countries, the question of whether or not immigrants should be allowed to practise female circumcision has been brought

---

4 Cf. Gellner (1978: 149): 'The United States is notorious for the way in which its educational system has acted as an agency for transforming ethnic groups into a culturally homogeneous mass, until it failed in our time to do the same for the coloured groups.'

up. In many countries, there is general agreement that ethnic distinctiveness is acceptable so long as it remains private – however, it is never easy to draw an unambiguous boundary between the private and the public. In several European countries, domestic violence is considered a public affair. Among many of the immigrants, the kin group alone is seen as responsible for handling such matters.

Conflicts of this kind can be studied as negotiations over the situational legitimacy of ethnic boundaries. Such conflicts can also be seen as *negotiations over meaning* involving different, culturally conditioned interpretations of social reality. Thus we see, again, that culture is far from irrelevant in ethnicity studies. As Roosens puts it: '[A]lthough ethnicity must be distinguished from "observable or objective" culture … it appears, paradoxically, as a privileged domain for the study of cultural dynamics' (Roosens, 1989: 161).

Minorities and modernity

Urban minorities and indigenous people are compelled to relate to majorities, to states, and to capitalist systems of production and consumption. The recodification or reification of culture and self-conscious assertion of identity displayed by some of them cannot be entirely divorced from this historical fact, and their ways of displaying their identities are confined to modern societies. Like nationalism, modern ethnic associations and networks seek to emulate a politically useful and emotionally satisfactory *Gemeinschaft* in an historical situation where such communities have to be *created* because they do not already exist. Similarly, certain political aspects of these minority–majority situations are specific to modern societies based on literacy, wagework, capitalism and the state.

The majority of ethnicity studies deal with modern societies or modernisation processes. The number of Sami in Norway in 1940 was not significantly lower than the number in 1990, but they were far less visible and lacked shared organisation and shared collective identity. In other words there was less Sami–Norwegian ethnicity, although it would be absurd to claim that there was 'less Sami culture'. The fact that indigenous peoples have more airtime, more organisations and more political influence does not mean that they acquire more members, but that their cultural integration into modernity and their visibility are greater. Thus they also take part in more interethnic relationships than previously.

A similar statement could be made with respect to urban migrants. The very fact that their migration is possible signifies that modernisation processes have taken place. Their displacement creates conditions for the articulation of ethnicity.

Despite the great political and cultural variations, there are interesting similarities between the ethnopolitical processes described in this and the previous chapter and the examples discussed in earlier chapters. Ethnic dichotomisation and boundary processes are implied in the very concept of ethnicity, and can be identified in all of the contexts presented. We should further note the general importance of fusing *political organisation* with the creation of a *collective identity* based on symbolic meaning in ethnic processes. These can be seen as two constitutive elements in ethnic organisation. If the San are eventually not successful in creating a politically relevant ethnic identity, they will try to pursue their goals in other ways than through ethnopolitics – possibly through individual social mobility, or through trade unionism.

As suggested in chapter 5, there are alternative ways in which ethnicity can be studied. Notably, a focus on economic processes could provide important background information accounting – at least in some cases – for the conditions in which ethnic identities form. Here, I have chosen to emphasise the inner logic of ethnic group and identity formation, seen as a process involving features of greater society, but frequently giving priority to the relationships between acting individuals. This does not necessarily make the analysis a voluntaristic one where, in the words of Worsley (1984: 246), life seems like a cafeteria. Of course, an individual San cannot choose whether or not he or she should be a San – that much is given. He or she cannot choose away the state either, or change the dominant mode of production in society, or his or her cultural background for that matter. Such parameters are important because they indicate the social and cultural framework within which people must act, but they do not enable us to predict *how* people will act (cf. Giddens, 1979; Bourdieu, 1977). In focusing on options, I have chiefly wished to call attention to the ambiguity of social situations, to the historical and situational relativity of ethnicity, and to the fact that people make history, although they do not do so under conditions of their own choice. Nor is it always clear to them whose history they are making.

In suggesting that people try to improve their situation, there is no implicit assumption about people acting from 'economic' motives. For the values people seek are culturally defined, and they do not always seem 'rational' from an economist's perspective. When a Trinidadian Hindu goes to perform *puja* at the local temple, or when a Jamaican in London attends a reggae concert, they may act that way because they find it inherently meaningful, not for political reasons. Only when someone is able to exploit the symbolism surrounding the *puja* or the concert for political ends, can it be exploited in ethnic organisation.

The final chapter of this book will illuminate the perspectives discussed previously through looking at that which is not ethnic. For ethnicity is created, and it is not only created by the people we study but also by ourselves. If a researcher looks for ethnicity, he or she will find it – possibly at the cost of missing out on other kinds of relationship which are also 'there'.

8 THAT WHICH IS NOT ETHNIC

Habit of seeing opposites. – The general imprecise way of observing sees everywhere in nature opposites (as, for example, 'warm and cold') where there are, not opposites, but differences in degree. This bad habit has led us into wanting to comprehend and analyse the inner world, too, the spiritual–moral world, in terms of such opposites. An unspeakable amount of pain, arrogance, harshness, estrangement, frigidity has entered into human feelings because we think we see opposites instead of transitions.

Friedrich Nietzsche (*Der Wanderer und sein Schatten*, § 67
(The Wanderer and his Shadow), 1988 [1880])

It is a feature of the contemporary world that groups and individuals apparently become more similar and more different at the same time. In Gellner's words, 'modern society is *both* more homogeneous *and* more diversified than those which preceded it' (Gellner, 1978: 141). Anthropological perspectives on ethnicity as process enable us to see this contradiction as a fundamental duality between similarity and difference, between inclusion and exclusion, between homogenisation and fragmentation. This book has emphasised that although people in a certain sense become more similar because of modernisation, they simultaneously become more distinctive, and that ethnicity is one principal expression of this diversification. Ethnic differentiation draws upon social, cultural and political resources which presuppose a prior institutionalisation of the contacts between the groups and their integration into a single system in certain respects. This, at least, is a way of stating in brief the orthodox anthropological position on ethnicity in the early 1990s. In this last chapter, I would like to move a few steps further in the light of recent research and theorising on social identity.

Changes in social theory

Most research on ethnicity implicitly presupposes that the nation-state is the 'pre-eminent power-container in our era', to use Giddens'

(1985) formulation. This is generally true of minority studies whether aboriginal or urban, studies of secessionist movements or 'proto-nations', or studies of power struggles or identity processes in 'plural societies'. Many social scientists have questioned this assumption in recent years, and argue that the world has changed in such a way that the nation-state is no longer an appropriate synonym for 'greater society'. Perhaps Eric Hobsbawm is correct when he attributes the currently great academic interest in nationalism to the Hegelian notion that 'the owl of Minerva flies at dusk' (Hobsbawm, 1990) – in other words, that the age of the nation-state is nearly over. And perhaps Ulf Hannerz (1989; 1992), Arjun Appadurai (1990) and other anthropologists are correct in suggesting that many contemporary men and women tend to seek their identifications and social alignments along different axes than was formerly the case – largely because capitalism and modern communications technology, from the satellite dish to the jet plane, have relativised the spatial dimension in human life. In Roland Robertson's somewhat hyperbolic phrase, the world has become a single place (Robertson, 1990).

Even more radical conclusions are arrived at by Anthony Giddens (1990; 1991) and Immanuel Wallerstein (1991b), who both argue the need for a profound rethinking of the categories of social science. In Wallerstein's view, the very concept of society has become obsolete – it may have been a useful nineteenth-century metaphor but, in his view, it is a misleading one in the seamless world system of the late twentieth century.

Starting from an opposite direction, several theorists have questioned the category of the individual. A common notion here is that individuals in the present world are less 'integrated' and somehow more transient and free-floating – situationally shifting, really – than was formerly the case. I refer to the theory of postmodernism or post-modernity (cf. Lash and Friedman, 1991; B. Turner, 1990). An interesting interpretation of this 'condition' is given by the social anthropologist Marilyn Strathern, who has argued that it is *our cultural fiction* of the integrated and bounded individual, who is presumed to be a member of 'a culture' and who lives his or her life as a continuous, directed person, which is about to lose its credibility (Strathern, 1992).

Much of this theorising seems to concern only a small, rich part of the world's population – bored urban secularised Western intellectuals and heavy consumers – however, the globalisation of culture and the relativisation of boundaries has a very widespread, if uneven, effect. At the time of the nuclear disaster in Chernobyl in 1986, I was on fieldwork in Mauritius and found that rural Indo-Mauritian cane-cutters discussed its consequences in the rum shop. Similarly, knowledge about possibilities for emigration to particular countries is widespread in many rural areas in poor countries – and everybody listens to American pop music. Unlike the globalisation of earlier times (from plantation economies onwards), this form of globalisation stimulates the emergence of a reflexive consciousness about the global system. In brief, many of the local communities of the world seem to become increasingly integrated into the global system on a political, economic and cultural level. In Mike Featherstone's words:

it may be possible to point to trans-societal processes which take on a variety of forms ... and processes which sustain the exchange and flow of goods, people, information, knowledge and images which give rise to communication processes which gain some autonomy on a global level. (Featherstone, 1990: 1)

Changes in the social world

Simultaneously, as noted in chapter 1, social identities in many parts of the world now seem to be more open to negotiation than they were in the decades following the Second World War. All over Europe, from Ireland and Norway to the Caucasus and Andalucia, there is in the early 1990s a lively discourse about which collective identities to attach oneself to. New nation-states have been formed and new minority problems arise. Old nation-states transfer some of their power to a new supranational unit, the European Union. New regionalist and ethnic movements emerge on both sides of the EU/EC boundary, and people are torn between what they see as the old and the new. Elsewhere in the world, there are also powerful ideological movements competing for people's adherence – politicised Islam in the Middle East, separatism and casteism in India, indigenous and 'ethnic minority' movements in North America, and so on. A great many of these movements share the crucial feature of appealing to people's sense of primordial bonds and cultural authenticity.

On the one hand, then, we witness powerful centripetal waves of cultural homogenisation, tighter economic integration (viz: the role of the World Bank and the International Monetary Fund in the poor countries), increasing participation in wagework and the monetary economy, increasing consumption of global cultural merchandise (from soap operas to Coca-Cola) and an increased flow of people to and from various destinations. The coming of satellite television creates conditions for simultaneity on a global scale: events may be witnessed anywhere no matter where they take place. 'Foreign is elsewhere!' exclaimed a nostalgic correspondent of *The Times* (UK) in April 1992, after having crossed the European continent without encountering what he thought of as cultural Otherness.

On the other hand, as we have seen, new 'localisms' – usually of an ethnic, religious or regional nature – continue to emerge and to assert their demands vis-à-vis the centres. As I have argued at length in earlier chapters, processes of modernisation or homogenisation are necessary conditions for these movements to develop and to articulate their demands effectively. As regards nationalism, the very idea of nationalism is a globalised one, which was developed in Europe and the European diaspora. Besides, social integration into wider systems is a condition for their identities to become relevant at all, since it is contact and not isolation that engenders social identity. This is obvious enough – the majority of the examples discussed in this book have indicated the importance of social change and contact with others for the emergence of new social identities. The question is nevertheless: what will such identities look like in the future?

Globalisation and localisation

Students of ethnic and national identities and ideologies are, if anything, at the centre of the theoretical and historical upheavals which I have alluded to. In a series of interrelated articles, Jonathan Friedman (1987; 1990; 1991) has proposed a research programme for a social anthropology which takes the challenge from postmodernity seriously. Friedman starts from the assumption that globalisation and localisation are two mutually dependent, interrelated processes. As Ulf Hannerz has argued in a similar context (Hannerz, 1990), cosmopolitans depend on locals in order to be able to conceive themselves to be, and to be regarded as, cosmopolitan. We may also add that perhaps it is true that the world is a single place – but if so, it is locally constructed. Notwithstanding migration and other globalising tendencies, people still live in places.

Friedman stresses that different inhabitants and groups of inhabitants in the world are in highly different structural and cultural positions, and that these differences must be elucidated. Sensing the imminence of a dramatic transformation, he describes the current situation like this:

It might seem difficult, if not wrong, to attempt to find unity in a world that is increasingly described in terms of fragmentation, disintegration, meaninglessness and cultural mix. I have tried, nevertheless, to locate the strands of what appears to be a single complex process of global transformation. This is not to say, of course, that there are no local structures, no autonomous cultural schemes, but that their orchestration occurs via a score whose principal theme is the decline of Western hegemony, which takes different forms in different parts of the global arena. Modernity moves east, leaving post-modernity in its wake; religious revival, ethnic renaissance, roots and nationalism are resurgent as modernist identity becomes increasingly futile in the West. In the structural confusion that characterizes the period, the periphery and margins of the system also react, in ... a complex combination of Third and Fourth World strategies. (Friedman, 1991: 360)

Friedman then outlines five major strategies, which he calls 'life-strategies, models for satisfying the structures of desire that emerge in the different niches of the global system' (ibid.).

The first is *modernist*. According to this view, society can be governed effectively on moral and sensible principles; and self, society and the world can develop according to presently conventional criteria.

The four remaining strategies build on the assumption that this kind of social and political identity is untenable because it has not delivered the goods. The first of these is plainly *postmodern* and can assume two, complementary shapes: a cynical distancing from all identification, but an acute awareness of the lack of identity; and a narcissistic dependence on consumption as a means for the presentation of self. A great number of critical analyses of modern society accuse capitalism and large-scale society of encouraging this fragmented, unpolitical and nihilistic kind of social identity – from philosophers like Marcuse (1964), via social analysts such as Berger (1977), Lasch (1980) and Sennett (1977), to historians of ideas such as Bloom (1987) and Finkielkraut (1987).

The next strategy is *traditionalist*. It can be religious and/or ethnic, and it includes many if not most of the ethnic and nationalist movements I have described in this book. According to Friedman, this kind of project is caused by an experienced need with individuals in modern societies to 'engage [themselves] in a larger project in which identity is concrete and fixed despite mobility, success and other external changes in social conditions' (Friedman, 1991: 361). Ecopolitical movements are related to these strategies (cf. Giddens, 1990, on 'green' traditionalism). Many ethnic movements may thus, within this analytical framework, be lumped with 'deep ecologists' and religious fundamentalists as 'traditionalists'. Although they frequently appear as anti-modern, modernity is a condition for their emergence.

The following strategy is labelled *Third World*, and is developed in order to attract wealth and power through clientship. Patron–client chains operate both domestically and internationally. Consumption is deemed important by the adherents of this strategy; the development of national infrastructure is abandoned.

The final strategy is called *Fourth World*, and is the strategy of 'exit from the system' – the formation of politically autonomous communities which aim at re-establishing a formerly repressed identity and lifestyle.

These five life-strategies are not mutually exclusive, but they do suggest (i) great qualitative variations within the global system, and (ii) that there *is* a global system which one has to relate to. In an earlier chapter, I stated that virtually every inhabitant of the world is forced to be a citizen. In line with globalisation theory, one might add that virtually everybody is forced to be a consumer in some way or other. Combinations of 'Third' and 'Fourth World' strategies seem common among indigenous peoples, who simultaneously strive for self-determination and for a higher material standard of living. Immigrant groups in Europe may combine 'traditionalist/ethnic/religious' and 'postmodern' strategies. Similarly, combinations of 'modernist' and 'postmodernist' strategies may be common in Western Europe, where people are simultaneously strongly concerned with their own lifestyle and the condition of their society.

What is remarkable about Friedman's (and others') contributions is the conviction that the world has indeed changed in such a way as to allow for other kinds of social alignments than those which were formerly viable. Some of these alignments will have an ethnic tag, others will not. The Islamic movement of the Middle East and North Africa can scarcely be considered an ethnic one. It aims at including a great number of peoples who are acknowledged to be culturally diverse. However, it has features which are similar to ethnic movements: it is anti-modernist and traditionalist, and it aims at a reconstitution of seemingly vanishing aspects of society, culture and identity.

Identities and loyalties

On the subject of segmentary identities, I.M. Lewis writes: 'A committed internationalist condemns parochial nationalism (little Englanderism) just as unequivocally as a nationalist condemns tribalism, a tribalist clannishness, and a clansman familism' (Lewis, 1985: 359). Since Evans-Pritchard's (1940) depiction of the segmentary lineage among the Nuer, this way of thinking has been with us in social anthropology. As we have seen in earlier chapters, this perspective on identity and groups can be very illuminating in ethnicity studies. We shall nevertheless move one step further. For Evans-Pritchard did not merely deal with the segmentary character of identities – political identities as concentric circles, so to speak – he also indicated that conflicting loyalties may reduce tensions and prevent conflicts between lineages.

The Nuer are patrilineal. If a sufficient number of Nuer men in lineage X have affines in lineage Y – either because they are married to women from lineage Y, or because their sisters are married to men from that lineage – this is a strong incentive not to start a feud with that lineage. If only a few men are so aligned, and the feud is a fact, the minority may experience conflicting loyalties – they may feel ill at ease whether they take part in the fighting or stay at home. Multiple or conflicting loyalties, moreover, do not only operate on the basis of kinship; enduring bonds are also formed on the basis of age-group fellowship, trade and personal friendship. According to Evans-Pritchard's own analysis, and particularly in Gluckman's (1982) use of his material, this criss-crossing web of conflicting loyalties seems to create a relatively stable social system among the potentially perennially warlike Nuer groupings.

In terms of ethnicity, multiple loyalties may be a problem for minorities, whose members may often be loyal to – and indeed members of – two ethnic groups or nations, or one ethnic group and one nation. But why ought this to be a problem? Clearly because the ideology of the nation-state remains hegemonic and the relationship between states is seen as one of potential conflict. Here, we should perhaps remember that the United *Nations* (sic) is an organisation of states which is generally not entitled to meddle in internal affairs. When Saddam Hussein entered Kuwait in August 1991, he broke the international rules; but when he tried out new chemical weapons on Iraqi Kurds, he did not.

Many people in the contemporary world are structurally placed so as to have multiple loyalties in ethnic terms. Apart from labour migrants, refugees and expatriates, transnational families are an obvious, increasingly common example. However, multiple loyalties need not follow ethnic lines. Kenneth Little (1978) has shown how gender loyalty – between women – can cut across ethnic lines in African societies, mitigate potential conflict and create problems for attempts at ethnic group formation. If women perceive that they have shared interests against the men, across ethnic boundaries, then their gender identity will situationally overrule the ethnic identity. Another basis for loyalty and identity can be social class membership. Even in Mauritius, where there is general agreement that the ethnic divisions are the most important ones, solidarity along class lines occasionally forms; in 1970 and in 1979 there were major strikes uniting Creoles, Hindus and Muslims against their employers. In this case, the class solidarity obviously overruled the ethnic solidarity, since several of the employers belonged to the same ethnic categories as the strikers.

In the contemporary world, social identities can form along several other lines as well. Employees of transnational companies are trained to be loyal to their company rather than their country, and many thousand may be assigned to appointments in foreign countries. Networks of professional solidarity are also transnational and cut across ethnic lines. An English anthropologist would definitely have something in common with an Indian anthropologist which she does not have in common with her neighbour. Rock enthusiasts from all over Western Europe gather at Reading and Glastonbury in Britain, at Roskilde in Denmark and at other major festivals during the summer. This kind of collective event obviously provides opportunities for the expression of shared identity. And we could go on. The question which must be asked pertains to whether or not ethnic identities are by default more 'basic' than others. Some would say yes, others would say no – and that is the state of the art.

We should stress here that multiple identities are not the same as segmentary identities. Multiple identities cannot be placed in concentric circles in orderly ways; they can scarcely be represented graphically at all. They cut across each other in the same manner as Sandra Wallman's open heterogeneous networks (see chapter 7): one has a shared identity with different people at different times. In this kind of social setting, the status sets of individuals are not clustered about intricate social relationships with a limited number of people; they are diverse and flexible.

Gender and ethnicity

In other words, non-ethnic identities and principles of social differentiation can be highly important. The relationship between class and ethnicity has already been discussed, particularly in chapters 3 and 5. *Gender* identity is arguably also of great social importance in every human society, although gender-based political organisations are comparatively rare. Just as recent research on ethnicity has indicated that ethnicity should be distinguished from culture, recent research on gender has argued that gender should not be seen as primarily biological, but rather as a cultural construction whose legitimacy is justified through references to biology (cf. Strathern, 1988: chs 1–2). According to these perspectives, gender is also most fruitfully seen as a social relation and not as an essence consisting of 'properties' or 'personality traits' – again, there are striking parallels with research on ethnicity.

The relationship between gender and ethnicity varies to such an extent, and can be so complex, that it would require another book to do justice to the subject. I shall therefore only give a bare outline of some central issues.

Sexual stereotyping is in many societies related to ethnicity in the sense that some ethnic categories of men (such as blacks in the United States) may have a reputation for sexual prowess and some categories of women similarly may have reputations as prudish or wanton. Gender imagery is often used to describe ethnic groups as a whole ('the Xs are effeminate'; 'the Ys are crude brutes with no manners', and so on).

In some societies in the Caribbean, there is a strong symbolic inter-relationship between class, ethnicity and gender in social classification. In Trinidad, the (emic) classificatory poles are African–Indian, male–female and working-class–middle-class. In general, women, Indians and members of the middle class are held to share certain char-acteristics – they are considered more 'respectable' than men, Africans and members of the working class, who are considered strong indi-vidualists with little sense of responsibility. If somebody does not turn up for an appointment, for example, this may be explained by referring to the fact that he is a man, an African and/or a member of the working class.

Regarding the structural position in society, there are interesting similarities between women in some societies and some indigenous groups to the extent that they are 'muted' categories (Ardener's, 1989c [1975] expression) with little formal power. Both oppressed women and oppressed indigenes are compelled to use the language of the dominators in order to be able to express their interests; neither has the power to define the terms of discourse. Both groups are taught that their specific social identity is immutable and (at least in the case of women) biological, and as a consequence that their subordination is 'natural'. Both groups may be told that their contribution to society is negligible and that they should therefore remain subordinated.

There is nevertheless a fundamental difference between gender systems and other systems of differentiation, including ethnicity. In every human society, there is an ideology to the effect that men and women need each other; that they are complementary. Ethnic minorities may be expelled, exterminated or ignored – women cannot be treated in the same way if the political leaders plan for societal continuity. Physical segregation along gender lines is also much more difficult to achieve than segregation along ethnic lines. In every society where it makes sense to talk of domestic and public fields of interaction, both genders will be represented in the domestic fields.

Some interesting perspectives on gender imagery in ethnic and nationalist ideology are discussed in Anthias and Yuval-Davies (1989), one of the few books which discuss the relationship between nationalism and gender (cf. Parker *et al.*, 1992). The contributors show that in so far as gender relations are made symbolically relevant in nationalist ideology, they tend to reproduce a patriarchal view of the family. If the nation is regarded as a metaphoric kin group, then the mother's metaphorical role must be to reproduce – to raise children and to provide domestic services. In war imagery, this passive role of women is particularly evident. 'The fathers have fought/and the mothers have wept' goes a famous line in the Norwegian national anthem. If the nation-state is symbolically depicted as a family writ large, then it makes sense to investigate actual family relations in the society in question to find the sources of nationalist imagery. Here we may find that nationalism tends to reproduce and strengthen the gender relations already prevalent in a society, albeit placing them at a more abstract level.

It can be about as difficult for a man to join a militant feminist group as it would be for him to change his ethnic membership in absolute terms. The point is not, therefore, that all notions of gender differences or cultural differences are pure inventions, but that every distinction – no matter how 'objective' or 'natural' it may seem to us – needs to be codified culturally in order to be recognised.

Beyond ethnicity?

Studies of ethnicity have tended to accentuate the enactment of boundary mechanisms and the use of overt markers of distinctiveness in the reproduction of ethnic identities. However, as we have seen, the social world can rarely be neatly divided into fixed groups with clear boundaries, unambiguous criteria for membership and an all-encompassing social relevance. Therefore, a one-sided focus on ethnicity may prevent a researcher from seeing social systems in other ways which may also be relevant.

First of all, the existence of ethnic anomalies or liminal categories should serve as a reminder that group boundaries are not unproblematic. These are groups or individuals who are 'betwixt and between', who are neither X nor Y and yet a bit of both. Their actual group membership may be open to situational negotiation, it may be ascribed by a dominant group, or the group may form a separate ethnic category.

Second, non-ethnic criteria for group membership are situationally relevant in every society, and in complex modern societies they proliferate and can be identified as multiple identities. Different forms of group loyalty and membership may be largely congruent with ethnic membership, or they may cut across it.

Is it still analytically fruitful to think about the social world in terms of ethnicity? Perhaps a wider term, such as 'social identity', would be more true to the flux and complexity of social processes, and would allow us to study group formation and alignments along a greater variety of axes than a single-minded focus on 'ethnicity' would. As Ulf Hannerz has stressed, cultural complexity combined with group differentiation is not necessarily linked with ethnicity. 'Complex societies have other kinds of interfaces between varieties of common sense, other kinds of marginality [as well as ethnicity]' (Hannerz, 1992: 133).

A problem concerning the concept of ethnicity is that it seems to imply that there exists *an ethnic phenomenon* (van den Berghe, 1981) in the world which requires a single explanation – which has biological or other shared and objective origins. We should be cautious of reifying the concept of ethnicity in this way. Rather, we would be well advised to follow Comaroff and Comaroff (1992: 54), who state that ethnicity 'describes both a set of relations and a mode of consciousness'. As a mode of consciousness, however, 'it is one among many ... each of which is produced as particular historical structures impinge themselves on human experience and condition social action' (ibid.).

A related question concerns the ways in which we think about ethnic boundaries. Several of the examples discussed in earlier chapters show that such boundaries are frequently ambiguous. In this regard, the theory of the plural society seems to be flawed in that it assumes, in a rather axiomatic way, that ethnic alignments are the most basic ones in polyethnic societies. It is not always obvious who is a member of a group and who is not, and it is not always obvious which kinds of groups count and which do not. We cannot assume a priori that ethnic alignments are more important than others.

Research on group formation and social identities has tended to regard groups as mutually exclusive in a *digital* way: either one is a member of X or one is not. I have nevertheless shown that people can often be *somewhat* X. The digital way of thinking about groups and identities may be influenced by nationalist ideology and practice, according to which one cannot simultaneously be and not be a citizen in a state. However, in real life people do not normally classify each other just by referring to their citizenship. Many other statuses are relevant. Therefore, it may, perhaps, be more appropriate to think of identity in general as an *analogic* phenomenon than as a *digital* one. Conceptualised in this way, degrees of sameness and difference, of inclusion and exclusion, may be identified. People may be a bit of this and a bit of that.

Empirically, social identities appear fluid, negotiable, situational, analogic (or gradualist) and segmentary. It is therefore an empirical question whether different identities are mutually exclusive, and certainly ethnic communities are social and cultural creations. As shown in previous chapters, identity is elastic and negotiable, but not infinitely flexible. Finally, it is a universal fact that not everybody can take part in a given community. All categorisations of group membership must have boundaries; they depend on *others* in order to make sense.

In my final empirical example, I shall outline a contemporary, social process where it may seem as if ethnicity is losing its relevance.

The end of ethnicity?

Whether or not ethnic identities become politically relevant depends on the wider social context. I have shown how ethnicity can assume different forms and may arise from different historical circumstances. I have argued that ethnic 'revitalisation' may be an inherent feature of modernity, and that many modernisation theorists who held that ethnic alignments were becoming obsolete, were wrong. However, we should also remember that, when all is said and done, ethnicity does not *necessarily* arise from modernity, and it is not necessarily an end-product.

The Mauritian labour market was traditionally strongly ethnically segregated.[1] Because of industrialisation (during and after the 1980s) and democratisation of the political system (from 1947 onwards), this segregation is in many areas giving way to a labour market recruiting its employees on the basis of individual merit rather than ethnic membership. A great number of the new factories and hotels are owned by foreigners with no ethnic commitments. Merit rather than connections becomes a criterion for recruitment.

Simultaneously, the democratisation of education is deepening. A growing number of Mauritians receive higher education abroad and later return to the island. Before independence, higher education was generally reserved for a handful of wealthy families. In the towns, people increasingly live in neighbourhoods appropriate to their class instead of ethnic neighbourhoods. Also, new venues for informal

---

1 The following ethnographic sketch draws on as yet unpublished material collected in Mauritius in 1986 and, chiefly, in 1991–2. Cf. also Eriksen (1988: ch. 5; 1992a).

social life appear: snackbars, new sports clubs, parties organised by the larger employers and so on. Most of these new arenas are not constituted on an ethnic basis.

From the individual Mauritian's point of view, his or her opportunities appear very different from what they would have been thirty years ago. Individual achievement is highly praised in official rhetoric. One can no longer rely on one's family. One competes as an individual on an equal footing with members of every 'community', including one's own. At school and at work, one encounters people from other ethnic categories and has important shared experiences with them.

From the societal perspective, industrial Mauritius is compelled to compete in the world market in unprecedented ways. Employees are thus being taught that their country's welfare depends on their achievement. The other groups relevant for one's own social identity therefore tend to become foreign states rather than domestic ethnic groups. Such a shift in identity focus, if it is successful, can be seen as an indication of an integration at a higher systemic level, where new sets of relationship are created. A good illustration of this was the spontaneous upsurge of nationalist sentiment in Mauritius following the international sports tournament Les Jeux des Iles de l'Océan Indien in 1985. Suddenly, dichotomisations between Mauritians and foreigners were becoming more relevant than those distinguishing Mauritians from each other (Eriksen, 1988: ch. 5).

There has been a perceptible growth in interethnic marriages. When the family has little to offer by way of material security, 'love marriages' become more viable than they were. What will be the identity of the children of such alliances? In many cases, the children are classified as 'some kind of Creoles', since the Creoles are regarded as a 'mixed' ethnic category. For many of these children, it would be a hopeless project to trace their genealogies and thereby establish their ancestry. There are individuals like the journalist who can count no less than nine different 'peoples' among his ancestors – from Brittany to Canton!

If the trend of interethnic marriages continues, an ultimate effect may be the end of ethnicity as we know it today. There will be too many 'anomalous' individuals around to maintain clear-cut distinctions. Loyalties may, as a consequence, be increasingly related to local history, culture and identities rather than to 'ancestral cultures'. Maybe the majority of Mauritians will regard their 'ancestral culture' as that mixture of influences which has shaped Mauritius. And perhaps a majority of the population will regard Kreol – the only language which grew out of the interethnic encounters in Mauritius – as their ancestral language. A woman of Tamil origin explains that her ancestral language was Kreol, since her parents as well as her grandparents spoke it, 'and as far as I'm concerned, they are ancestral enough'. (How many generations must one go back in time in order to establish one's 'ancestry'? This, of course, is socially defined.)

This kind of scenario is possible but not inevitable. Calls for religious purity are common and new traditionalist movements are being formed, particularly in the countryside. The leaders of these movements rail against what they see as the decadence associated with urbanism, modernity and cultural homogenisation or 'Creolisation'. The potential appeal of such movements depends on what they have to offer. If they can convince a sufficiently large number of people that they offer economic security and/or personal integrity, they may be successful. However, such a 'new wave of ethnicity' may divide the Mauritian population along unfamiliar lines, since its main base will probably be the countryside. The rural/urban or industrial/agricultural opposition may become more salient than the Creole/Hindu dichotomy.

There are two chief factors militating against the fusion of ethnic categories. First, the family is still important in Mauritius, and parents are not likely to encourage mixed marriages. Second, religion is a strong factor in boundary maintenance. If the parties to an interethnic marriage practise different religions, the chances that the marriage will endure are relatively slim. The majority of stable mixed marriages involve couples who either belong to the same religion (by birth or by conversion) or for whom religion does not play an important part in their lives.

In addition, many Mauritians dislike the idea of the disappearance of distinctive 'cultures'. 'Keep the colours of the Mauritian rainbow distinct, and it will remain beautiful,' was the advice of the Catholic Archbishop of Mauritius at a meeting in 1991.

If it is easy to discern the end of ethnicity in persons, social contexts and the social structure of Mauritius, it is almost as easy to discover ethnic revitalisation. That, in fact, is what many anthropologists studying social change have done in various societies. Movements of ethnic revitalisation are much more spectacular than the quiet daily movement towards mutual accommodation in complex societies, and they are perhaps therefore more attractive as objects of study. This does not, however, necessarily mean that such movements are more representative than moves towards the end of ethnicity in particular societies. After all, seen through the perspective of *la longue durée*, the eventual disappearance of ethnic groups is no less certain than their appearance.

The eye of the beholder

During the heyday of Marxist social science in the 1970s, numerous well-researched studies were published on classic 'plural societies' such as the US, Mauritius, Trinidad and Malaysia. Many of these studies seemed to show unequivocally that ethnic conflict and ethnic identity were surface phenomena which were ultimately determined by domestic class relations or by international imperialism. Few would argue in the same manner twenty years later, although the societies themselves may not have changed profoundly. This should serve as a reminder that the choice of an analytical perspective or 'research hypothesis' is not an innocent act. If one goes out to look for ethnicity, one will 'find' it and thereby contribute to constructing it. For this reason, a concern with non-ethnic dimensions of polyethnic societies can be a healthy corrective and supplement to analyses of ethnicity.

The anthropological interest in ethnicity is not universal. In French anthropology, the concept of *ethnicité* has never caught on in the same way as the word ethnicity has in British and American anthropology (A-C. Taylor, 1991). The connotations of *ethnie* ('ethnic group') in French are sometimes uncomfortably close to obsolete notions of race or reifying notions of 'cultures'. This does not merely concern a difference in the choice of words; differences in terminology may (as we have seen in the case of ethnic labels) indicate differences in epistemology. When mainstream French anthropologists study what we would speak of as political ethnicity, they may subsume it under the study of politics in general; when concerned with ethnic identity processes and ideology, they may connect these issues with studies of identity and ideology in general (for example, Lévi-Strauss, 1977), rather than assuming that there is such a thing as an 'ethnic phenomenon' which merits elevation to the status of a comparative concept. Thus, in Pierre Bonté's and Michel Izard's massive *Dictionnaire de l'ethnologie et de l'anthropologie* (Bonté and Izard, 1991), there is no entry on *ethnicité*, but the subject is briefly treated under keywords such as *ethnie* and *ethnies minoritaires*. This difference should remind us that when all is said and done, ethnicity is a social and cultural product which anthropologists contribute to creating. If we go to Mauritius, the Copperbelt or to the Peruvian highlands in search of gender, we shall no doubt find gender; the same holds good for, say, class, ideology and kinship systems. This reservation does not mean that the concept of ethnicity is not useful, however.

A focus on ethnic processes enables us to investigate topics which are of crucial importance in social anthropology: the relationship between culture, identity and social organisation; the relationship between meaning and politics; the multivocality of symbols; social processes of classification; the relationships between action and structure, structure and process, and continuity and change. Research on ethnicity has opened up exciting new fields in social anthropology, and it still has much to offer. Nonetheless, we ought to be critical enough to abandon the concept of ethnicity the moment it becomes a straitjacket rather than a tool for generating new understanding.

BIBLIOGRAPHY

Anderson, Benedict (1991 [1983]) *Imagined Communities. Reflections on the Origins and Spread of Nationalism*, 2nd edition. London: Verso

Anthias, Flora & Nira Yuval-Davies, eds. (1989) *Woman – Nation – State*. London: Macmillan

Appadurai, Arjun (1990) 'Disjuncture and difference in the global world economy'. In Mike Featherstone, ed., *Global Culture: Nationalism, Globalization and Modernity*, pp. 295–310. London: Sage

Archetti, Eduardo P. (1991) 'Masculinity and soccer: the formation of national identity in Argentina.' Paper presented at the American Ethnological Society spring meeting, Charleston, SC, USA, 14–16 March 1991.

Ardener, Edwin (1989a [1972]) 'Language, ethnicity and population'. In Edwin Ardener, *The Voice of Prophecy and Other Essays*, ed. Malcolm Chapman, pp. 65–71. Oxford: Blackwell

—— (1989b [1974]) 'Social anthropology and population'. In Edwin Ardener, *The Voice of Prophecy and Other Essays*, ed. Malcolm Chapman, pp. 109–27. Oxford: Blackwell

—— (1989c [1975]) 'Belief and the problem of women'. In Edwin Ardener, *The Voice of Prophecy and Other Essays*, ed. Malcolm Chapman, pp. 72–85. Oxford: Blackwell

Arens, William (1978) *The Man-eating Myth: Anthropology and Anthropophagy*. Oxford: Oxford University Press

Bailey, F.G. (1968) 'Parapolitical systems'. In M.J. Swartz, ed., *Local-level Politics. Social and Cultural Perspectives*, pp. 281–93. Chicago: Aldine

Balibar, Etienne (1991) 'Class racism'. In Etienne Balibar and Immanuel Wallerstein, *Race, Nation, Class: Ambiguous Identities*, pp. 204–16. London: Verso

Banton, Michael (1967) *Race Relations*. London: Tavistock

—— (1983) *Racial and Ethnic Competition*. Cambridge: Cambridge University Press

—— (1987) *Racial Theories*. Cambridge: Cambridge University Press

Barth, Fredrik (1956) 'Ecological relations of ethnic groups in Swat, north Pakistan'. *American Anthropologist*, vol. 58 (6), pp. 1079–89

—— (1969a) 'Introduction'. In Fredrik Barth, ed., *Ethnic Groups and Boundaries. The Social Organization of Culture Difference*, pp. 9–38. Oslo: Universitetsforlaget (Scandinavian University Press)

——, ed. (1969b) *Ethnic Groups and Boundaries. The Social Organization of Culture Difference*. Oslo: Universitetsforlaget (Scandinavian University Press)

Bateson, Gregory (1979) *Mind and Nature: A Necessary Unity*. Glasgow: Fontana

Benedict, Burton (1965) *Mauritius: Problems of a Plural Society*. London: Pall Mall

Benoist, Jean-Marie (1977) 'Facettes de l'identité'. In Claude Lévi-Strauss, ed., *L'Identité*, pp. 13–23. Paris: Presses Universitaires Françaises

Bentley, G. Carter (1987) 'Ethnicity and practice'. *Comparative Studies in Society and History*, vol. 29 (1), pp. 24–55

Berger, Peter (1977) *Facing up to Modernity*. New York: Basic Books

Berman, Marshall (1982) *All That is Solid Melts into Air: The Experience of Modernity*. London: Verso

Berthelsen, Christian (1990) 'Greenlandic in schools'. In Dirmid R.F. Collis, ed., *Arctic Languages: An Awakening*, pp. 333–40. Paris: Unesco

Birch, Anthony H. (1989) *Nationalism and National Integration*. London: Unwin Hyman

Blom, Jan-Petter (1969) 'Ethnic and cultural differentiation'. In Fredrik Barth, ed., *Ethnic Groups and Boundaries. The Social Organization of Culture Difference*, pp. 75–85. Oslo: Universitetsforlaget (Scandinavian University Press)

Bloom, Allan (1987) *The Closing of the American Mind*. New York: Simon & Schuster

Bonté, Pierre and Michel Izard, eds. (1991) *Dictionnaire de l'ethnologie et de l'anthropologie*. Paris: Presses Universitaires Françaises

✓ Bourdieu, Pierre (1977) *Outline of a Theory of Practice*, tr. Richard Nice. Cambridge: Cambridge University Press

Brass, Paul, ed. (1985) *Ethnic Groups and the State*. London: Croom Helm

Brereton, Bridget (1979) *Race Relations in Colonial Trinidad 1870–1900*. Cambridge: Cambridge University Press

Bromley, Yuri (1974) 'The term "ethnos" and its definition'. In Yuri Bromley, ed., *Soviet Ethnology and Anthropology Today*, pp. 55–72. The Hague: Mouton

Bulmer, Ralph (1967) 'Why is the cassowary not a bird? A problem of zoological taxonomy among the Karam of the New Guinea highlands'. *Man*, vol. 2 (1), pp. 5–25

Caistor, Nick (1992) 'Whose war is it anyway? The Argentine press during the South Atlantic conflict'. In James Aulich, ed., *Framing the Falklands War. Nationhood, Culture and Identity*, pp. 50–7. Milton Keynes: Open University Press

Chagnon, Napoleon (1983) *Yanomamö. The Fierce People*, 3rd edition. New York: Holt, Rinehart & Winston

Chapman, Malcolm, Maryon McDonald and Elizabeth Tonkin (1989) 'Introduction – history and social anthropology'. In Elizabeth Tonkin, Maryon

McDonald and Malcolm Chapman, eds., *History and Ethnicity*, pp. 1–21. London: Routledge

Cohen, Abner (1969) *Custom and Politics in Urban Africa*. London: Routledge

—— (1974a) 'Introduction: the lesson of ethnicity'. In Abner Cohen, ed., *Urban Ethnicity*, pp. ix–xxii. London: Tavistock

—— (1974b) *Two-dimensional Man*. London: Tavistock

—— (1981) *The Politics of Elite Culture: Explorations in the Dramaturgy of Power in a Modern African Society*. Berkeley, Calif.: University of California Press

Cohen, Ronald (1978) 'Ethnicity: Problem and focus in anthropology', *Annual Review of Anthropology*, vol. 7, pp. 379–404

Comaroff, John and Jean Comaroff (1992) *Ethnography and the Historical Imagination*. Boulder, Colo.: Westview

Connor, Walker (1978) 'A nation is a nation, is a state, is an ethnic group, is a ...' *Ethnic and Racial Studies*, vol. 1 (4), pp. 378–400

Cox, Oliver (1976) *Race Relations: Elements and Social Dynamics*. Detroit, Mich.: Wayne State University Press

Dahya, Badr (1974) 'The nature of Pakistani ethnicity in industrial cities in Britain'. In Abner Cohen, ed., *Urban Ethnicity*, pp. 77–118. London: Tavistock

De Vos, George and Lola Romanucci-Ross, eds. (1975) *Ethnic Identity: Cultural Communities and Change*. Palo Alto, Calif.: Mayfield

Despres, Leo (1975a) 'Ethnicity and resource competition in Guyanese society'. In Leo A. Despres, ed. *Ethnicity and Resource Competition in Plural Societies*, pp. 87–118. The Hague: Mouton

—— , ed. (1975b) *Ethnicity and Resource Competition in Plural Societies*. The Hague: Mouton

Douglas, Mary (1966) *Purity and Danger*. London: Routledge

—— (1970) *Natural Symbols*. London: Barrie & Rockliff

Dumont, Louis (1992) *L'Idéologie allemande*. Paris: Seuil

Durkheim, Emile and Marcel Mauss (1964 [1903]) *Primitive Classification*, tr. Rodney Needham. London: Cohen & West

Duroselle, Jean-Baptiste (1990) *Europe – A History of its Peoples*. Harmondsworth: Penguin

Eidheim, Harald (1969) 'When ethnic identity is a social stigma'. In Fredrik Barth, ed., *Ethnic Groups and Boundaries. The Social Organization of Culture Difference*, pp. 39–57. Oslo: Universitetsforlaget (Scandinavian University Press)

—— (1971) *Aspects of the Lappish Minority Situation*. Oslo: Universitetsforlaget (Scandinavian University Press)

—— (1992) *Stages in the Development of Sami Selfhood*. Dept. of Social Anthropology, University of Oslo: working paper no. 7

Epstein, A.L (1958) *Politics in an Urban African Community*. Manchester: Manchester University Press

—— (1978) *Ethos and Identity: Three Studies in Ethnicity*. London: Tavistock

—— (1992) *Scenes from African Urban Life. Collected Copperbelt Essays*. Edinburgh: Edinburgh University Press

Eriksen, Thomas H. (1986) 'Creole culture and social change'. *Journal of Mauritian Studies*, vol. 1 (2), pp. 59–72

—— (1988) *Communicating Cultural Difference and Identity. Ethnicity and Nationalism in Mauritius*. Oslo: Dept. of Social Anthropology, University of Oslo, occasional papers in social anthropology

—— (1990) 'Linguistic diversity and the quest for national identity: the case of Mauritius'. *Ethnic and Racial Studies*, vol. 13 (1), pp. 1–24

—— (1991a) 'The cultural contexts of ethnic differences'. *Man*, vol. 26 (1), pp. 127–44

—— (1991b) 'Ethnicity versus nationalism'. *Journal of Peace Research*, vol. 28 (3), pp. 263–78

—— (1991c) *Languages at the Margins of Modernity: Linguistic Minorities and the Nation-state*. Oslo: International Peace Research Institute (PRIO), PRIO report no. 5, 1991

—— (1992a) *Us and Them in Modern Societies: Ethnicity and Nationalism in Trinidad, Mauritius and Beyond*. Oslo: Scandinavian University Press

—— (1992b) 'Multiple traditions and the problem of cultural integration'. *Ethnos*, vol. 57 (1–2), pp. 5–30

Evans-Pritchard, E.E. (1940) *The Nuer*. Oxford: Clarendon Press

Fallers, Lloyd A. (1974) *The Social Anthropology of the Nation-State*. Chicago: Aldine

Fardon, Richard (1987) '"African ethnogenesis": limits to the comparability of ethnic phenomena'. In Ladislav Holy, ed., *Comparative Anthropology*, pp. 168–88. Oxford: Blackwell

Featherstone, Mike (1990) 'Global culture: an introduction'. In Mike Featherstone, ed., *Global Culture. Nationalism, Globalization and Modernity*, pp. 1–14. London: Sage

Feit, Harvey (1985) 'Legitimation and autonomy in James Bay – Cree responses to hydro-electric development'. In Noel Dyck, ed., 'Indigenous peoples and the nation-state'. St Johns, Newfoundland: Memorial University of Newfoundland papers, no. 14, pp. 27–60

Finkielkraut, Alain (1987) *La Défaite de la pensée*. Paris: Gallimard

Fishman, Joshua A. (1989) *Language and Ethnicity in Minority Sociolinguistic Perspective*. Philadelphia, Penn.: Multilingual Matters

—— *et al.* (1966) *Language Loyalty in the United States*. The Hague: Mouton

Forsythe, Diana (1989) 'German identity and the problem of history'. In Elizabeth Tonkin, Maryon McDonald and Malcolm Chapman, eds., *History and Ethnicity*, pp. 137–56. London: Routledge

Friedman, Jonathan (1987) 'Prolegomena to the adventures of Phallus in Blunderland: An anti-anti discourse'. *Culture and History*, no. 1, pp. 31–49

—— (1990) 'Being in the world: globalization and localization'. In Mike Featherstone, ed., *Global Culture*, pp. 311–28. London: Sage

—— (1991) 'Narcissism, roots and postmodernity: the constitution of selfhood in the global crisis'. In Scott Lash and Jonathan Friedman, eds., *Modernity and Identity*, pp. 331–66. Oxford: Blackwell

Furnivall, J.S. (1948) *Colonial Policy and Practice: A Comparative Study of Burma and Netherlands India*. Cambridge: Cambridge University Press

Geertz, Clifford (1973 [1963]) 'The integrative revolution: primordial sentiments and civil politics in the new states'. In Clifford Geertz, *The Interpretation of Cultures*, pp. 255–310. New York: Basic Books

Gellner, Ernest (1964) *Thought and Change*. London: Weidenfeld & Nicolson

—— (1978) 'Scale and nation'. In Fredrik Barth, ed., *Scale and Social Organization*, pp. 133–49. Oslo: Universitetsforlaget (Scandinavian University Press)

—— (1983) *Nations and Nationalism*. Oxford: Blackwell

—— (1991) 'Le Nationalisme en apesanteur'. *Terrain*, no. 17, pp. 7–16

Giddens, Anthony (1979) *Central Problems in Social Theory*. London: Macmillan

—— (1984) *The Constitution of Society*. Cambridge: Polity

—— (1985) *The Nation-state and Violence*. Cambridge: Polity

—— (1990) *The Consequences of Modernity*. Cambridge: Polity

—— (1991) *Modernity and Self-identity*. Cambridge: Polity

Glazer, Nathan and Daniel A. Moynihan (1963) *Beyond the Melting-pot*. Cambridge, Mass.: Harvard University Press

——, eds. (1975) *Ethnicity: Theory and Experience*. Cambridge, Mass.: Harvard University Press

Gluckman, Max (1961) 'Anthropological problems arising from the African industrial revolution'. In Aidan Southall, ed., *Social Change in Modern Africa*, pp. 67–83. London: Oxford University Press

—— (1982 [1956]) *Conflict and Custom in Africa*. Oxford: Blackwell

Goffman, Erving (1959) *The Presentation of Self in Everyday Life*. New York: Doubleday

Goody, Jack (1977) *The Domestication of the Savage Mind*. Cambridge: Cambridge University Press

Grillo, Ralph (1980) 'Introduction'. In Ralph Grillo, ed., *'Nation' and 'State' in Europe*. London: Academic Press

Grønhaug, Reidar (1974) *Micro-Macro Relations. Social Organization in Antalya, Southern Turkey*. Bergen: Bergen Studies in Social Anthropology, no. 7

Gulbrandsen, Ørnulf (1992) 'On the problem of egalitarianism: the Kalahari San in transition'. In Reidar Grønhaug, Gunnar Haaland and Georg Henriksen, eds., *The Ecology of Choice and Symbols. Essays in Honour of Fredrik Barth*, pp. 81–110. Bergen: Alma Mater

Haaland, Gunnar (1969) 'Economic determinants in ethnic processes'. In Fredrik Barth, ed., *Ethnic Groups and Boundaries. The Social Organization of Culture Difference*, pp. 58–74. Oslo: Universitetsforlaget (Scandinavian University Press)

—— (1992) 'Cultural content and ethnic boundaries'. In Reidar Grønhaug, Gunnar Haaland and Georg Henriksen, eds., *The Ecology of Choice and Symbols. Essays in Honour of Fredrik Barth*, pp. 155–79. Bergen: Alma Mater

Handelman, Don (1977) 'The organization of ethnicity'. *Ethnic Groups*, vol. 1, pp. 187–200

Handler, Richard (1988) *Nationalism and the Politics of Culture in Quebec*. Madison, Wisc.: Wisconsin University Press

—— and Daniel Segal (1992) 'How European is nationalism?' *Social Analysis*, vol. 32, pp. 1–15

Hannerz, Ulf (1980) *Exploring the City: Inquiries Toward and Urban Anthropology*. New York: Columbia University Press

—— (1989) 'Notes on the global ecumene'. *Public Culture*, vol. 1 (2), pp. 66–75

—— (1990) 'Cosmopolitans and locals in world culture'. In Mike Featherstone, ed., *Global Culture. Nationalism, Globalization and Modernity*, pp. 237–52. London: Sage

—— (1992) *Cultural Complexity: Studies in the Social Organization of Meaning*. New York: Columbia University Press

Heiberg, Marianne (1989) *The Making of the Basque Nation*. Cambridge: Cambridge University Press

Henriksen, Georg (1992) 'The experience of social worth as a force in inter-ethnic relations'. In Reidar Grønhaug, Gunnar Haaland and Georg Henriksen, eds., *The Ecology of Choice and Symbols. Essays in Honour of Fredrik Barth*, pp. 407–25. Bergen: Alma Mater

Herzfeld, Michael (1987) *Anthropology through the Looking-glass. Critical Ethnography in the Margins of Europe*. Cambridge: Cambridge University Press

Hirschmann, Alfred O. (1970) *Exit, Voice, Loyalty: Responses to Decline in Firms, Organizations and States*. Cambridge, Mass.: Harvard University Press

Hobsbawm, Eric (1977) 'Some reflections on "The Break-up of Britain"'. *New Left Review*, no. 105, pp. 3–23

—— (1983) 'Introduction: inventing traditions'. In Eric Hobsbawm and Terence Ranger, eds., *The Invention of Tradition*, pp. 1–14. Cambridge: Cambridge University Press

—— (1990) *Nations and Nationalism since the 1780s: Programme, Myth, Reality*. Cambridge: Cambridge University Press

Holy, Ladislav and Milan Stuchlik (1983) *Actions, Norms and Representations: Foundations of Anthropological Inquiry*. Cambridge: Cambridge University Press

Horowitz, Donald L. (1985) *Ethnic Groups in Conflict*. Berkeley, Calif.: University of California Press

Howell, Signe and Roy Willis, eds. (1989) *Societies at Peace*. London: Routledge

Jenkins, Richard (1986) 'Social anthropological models of inter-ethnic relations'. In John Rex and David Mason, eds., *Theories of Race and Race Relations*, pp. 170–86. Cambridge: Cambridge University Press

Joyce, James (1984 [1922]) *Ulysses*. Harmondsworth: Penguin

Just, Roger (1989) 'Triumph of the ethnos'. In Elizabeth Tonkin, Maryon McDonald and Malcolm Chapman, eds., *History and Ethnicity*, pp. 71–88. London: Routledge

Kapferer, Bruce (1988) *Legends of People, Myths of State. Violence, Intolerance and Political Culture in Sri Lanka and Australia*. Washington, DC: Smithsonian Institute Press

—— (1989) 'Nationalist ideology and a comparative anthropology'. *Ethnos*, vol. 54, pp. 161–99

Kelly, Aidan J.D. (1989) 'Ethnic identification, association and redefinition: Muslim Pakistanis and Greek Cypriots in Britain'. In Karmela Liebkind, ed., *New Identities in Europe: Immigrant Ancestry and the Ethnic Identity of Youth*, pp. 77–115. Aldershot: Gower

Klass, Morton (1991) *Singing with Sai Baba: The Politics of Revitalization in Trinidad*. Boulder, Colo.: Westview

Kroeber, A.L. and Clyde Kluckhohn (1952) *Culture: A Critical Review of Concepts and Definitions*. Cambridge, Mass.: Harvard University Press

Kuper, Adam (1988) *The Invention of Primitive Society. Transformations of an Illusion*. London: Routledge

Kuter, Lois (1989) 'Breton vs. French: language and the opposition of political, economic, social and cultural values'. In Nancy Dorian, ed., *Investigating Obsolescence. Studies in Language Contraction and Death*, pp. 75–90. Cambridge: Cambridge University Press

La Piere, R. (1934) 'Attitudes versus actions'. *Social Forces*, vol. 13, pp. 230–7

Lal, Barbara Ballis (1986) 'The "Chicago School" of American sociology, symbolic interactionism, and race relations theory'. In David Mason and John Rex, eds., *Theories of Race and Ethnic Relations*, pp. 280–99. Cambridge: Cambridge University Press

Lasch, Christopher (1980) *The Culture of Narcissism*. London: Abacus

Lash, Scott and Jonathan Friedman, eds. (1991) *Modernity and Identity*. Oxford: Blackwell

Leach, Edmund R. (1954) *Political Systems of Highland Burma*. London: Athlone

Leman, Johan (1987) *From Challenging Culture to Challenged Culture: The Sicilian Cultural Code and the Socio-cultural Praxis of Sicilian Immigrants in Belgium*. Leuven: Leuven University Press

Lévi-Strauss, Claude (1962) *La Pensée sauvage*. Paris: Plon. [English edition: *The Savage Mind*, University of Chicago Press, 1966]

——, ed. (1977) *L'Identité*. Paris: Presses Universitaires Françaises

Lewis, I.M. (1985) *Social Anthropology in Perspective: The Relevance of Social Anthropology*, 2nd edition. Cambridge: Cambridge University Press

Liebkind, Karmela , ed. (1989) *New Identities in Europe*. Aldershot: Gower

Little, Kenneth (1978) 'Countervailing influences in African ethnicity: a less apparent factor'. In Brian du Toit, ed., *Ethnicity in Modern Africa*, pp. 175–89 Boulder, Colo.: Sage

Lock, Margaret (1990) 'On being ethnic: the politics of identity breaking and making in Canada, or, *Nevra* on Sunday'. *Culture, Medicine and Psychiatry*, vol. 14, pp. 237–54

McDonald, Maryon (1989) *'We are not French!' Language, Culture and Identity in Brittany*. London: Routledge

Marcuse, Herbert (1964) *One-dimensional Man: Studies in the Ideology of Advanced Industrial Society.* Boston, Mass.: Beacon Press

Maybury-Lewis, David (1984) 'Living in Leviathan: ethnic groups and the state'. In David Maybury-Lewis, ed., *The Prospects for Plural Societies,* pp. 220–31. Washington, DC: American Ethnological Society

Mayer, Philip (1961) *Tribesmen or Townsmen: Conservatism and the Process of Urbanization in a South African City.* Cape Town: Oxford University Press

Minority Rights Group (1990) *World Directory of Minorities.* London: Longman

Mitchell, J. Clyde (1956) *The Kalela Dance.* Manchester: Manchester University Press, Rhodes-Livingstone papers, no. 27

—— (1966) 'Theoretical orientations in African urban studies'. In Michael Banton, ed., *The Social Anthropology of Complex Societies,* pp. 37–68. London: Tavistock

—— (1974) 'Perceptions of ethnicity and ethnic behaviour: an empirical exploration'. In Abner Cohen, ed., *Urban Ethnicity,* pp. 1–26. London: Tavistock

Mittelholzer, Edgar (1979 [1950]) *A Morning at the Office.* London: Heinemann

Moerman, Michael (1965) 'Who are the Lue: ethnic identification in a complex civilization'. *American Anthropologist,* vol. 67, pp. 1215–29

Naipaul, V.S. (1969) *The Loss of El Dorado.* London: André Deutsch

—— (1973) *The Overcrowded Barracoon.* Harmondsworth: Penguin

Nairn, Tom (1977) *The Break-up of Britain.* London: New Left Books

Nash, Manning (1988) *The Cauldron of Ethnicity in the Modern World.* Chicago: Chicago University Press

Neumann, Iver B. and Jennifer M. Welsh (1991) 'The Other in European Self-definition. A Critical Addendum to the Literature on International Society'. *Review of International Studies,* vol. 17(4), pp. 327–48

Nietzsche, Friedrich (1988 [1880]) *A Nietzsche Reader,* ed. and trans. R.J. Hollingdale. Harmondsworth: Penguin

Novak, Michael (1971) *The Rise of the Unmeltable Ethnics.* New York: Macmillan

O'Brien, Jay (1986) 'Toward a reconstitution of ethnicity: capitalist expansion and cultural dynamics in Sudan'. *American Anthropologist,* vol. 88, pp. 898–906

Okamura, Jonathan (1981) 'Situational ethnicity'. *Ethnic and Racial Studies,* vol. 4, pp. 452–63

Okely, Judith (1983) *The Traveller-Gypsies.* Cambridge: Cambridge University Press

Paine, Robert, ed. (1971) 'Patrons and brokers in the east Arctic'. St Johns, Newfoundland: Memorial University of Newfoundland, social and economic papers, no. 2

—— (1985) 'Ethnodrama and the "Fourth World": The Saami action group in Norway'. Memorial University of Newfoundland, social and economic papers, no. 14

—— (1992) 'The claim to aboriginality: Saami in Norway'. In Reidar Grønhaug, Gunnar Haaland and Georg Henriksen, eds., *The Ecology of Choice and Symbols. Essays in Honour of Fredrik Barth*, pp. 388–407. Bergen: Alma Mater

Park, Robert E. (1950) *Race and Culture*. Glencoe, Ill.: Free Press

—— (1955 [1921]) 'Sociology and the social sciences'. In Robert E. Park, *Society, Collective Behaviour, News and Opinion, Sociology and Modern Society*. Glencoe, Ill.: Free Press

Parker, Andrew, Mary Russo, Doris Sommer and Patricia Yaeger, eds. (1992) *Nationalism & Sexualities*. London: Routledge

Parkin, David (1974) 'Congregational and interpersonal ideologies in political ethnicity'. In Abner Cohen, ed., *Urban Ethnicity*, pp. 119–57. London: Tavistock

Patterson, Orlando (1977) *Ethnic Chauvinism. The Reactionary Impulse*. New York: Stein & Day

Peel, J.D.Y. (1989) 'The cultural work of Yoruba ethnogenesis'. In Elizabeth Tonkin, Maryon McDonald and Malcolm Chapman, eds., *History and Ethnicity*, pp. 198–215. London: Routledge

Pryce, Ken (1979) *Endless Pressure. A Study of West Indian Life-styles in Bristol*. Bristol: Bristol Classical Press

Renan, Ernest (1992 [1882]) *Qu'est-ce qu'une nation?* Paris: Presses Pocket

Rex, John (1973) *Race, Colonialism and the City*. London: Routledge

—— and David Mason, eds. (1986) *Theories of Race and Ethnic Relations*. Cambridge: Cambridge University Press

—— and Robert Moore (1967) *Race, Community and Conflict: A Study of Sparkbrook*. Oxford: Oxford University Press

Robertson, Roland (1990) 'Mapping the global condition: globalization as the central concept'. In Mike Featherstone, ed., *Global Culture. Nationalism, Globalization and Modernity*, pp. 15–30. London: Sage

Roosens, Eugeen E. (1989) *Creating Ethnicity*. London: Sage

Rosaldo, Michelle Z. (1984) 'Towards an anthropology of self and feeling'. In Richard A. Shweder and Robert LeVine, eds., *Culture Theory*, pp. 137–54. Cambridge: Cambridge University Press

Rushdie, Salman (1991) *Imaginary Homelands*. London: Granta

Sartre, Jean-Paul (1943) *L'Être et le néant*. Paris: Gallimard

Sennett, Richard (1977) *The Fall of Public Man*. New York: Knopf

Shils, Edward (1980) *Tradition*. Glencoe, Ill.: Free Press

Sjöberg, Katarina (1990) 'Mr. Ainu'. Ph.D. thesis, Dept. of Anthropology, University of Lund

Smith, Anthony D. (1986) *The Ethnic Origin of Nations*. Oxford: Blackwell

—— (1992) 'National identity and the idea of European unity'. *International Affairs*, vol. 68 (1), pp. 55–76

Smith, M.G. (1965) *The Plural Society of The British West Indies*. London: Sangster's

—— (1984) *Culture, Race and Class in the Commonwealth Caribbean*. Mona, Jamaica: Institute of Social and Economic Research (ISER)

Sniderman, Paul M. and Michael Gray Hagen (1985) *Race and Inequality. A Study in American Values*. Chatham, NJ: Chatham House

Southall, Aidan (1970) 'The illusion of tribe'. *Journal of Asian and African Studies*, vol. 5, pp. 28–50

—— (1976) 'Nuer and Dinka are people: ecology, ethnicity and logical possibility'. *Man*, vol. 11 (4), pp. 463–91

Steinberg, Stephen (1981) *The Ethnic Myth: Race, Ethnicity and Class in America*. New York: Atheneum

Stewart, Michael (1991) 'Un peuple sans patrie'. *Terrain*, no. 17, pp. 39–52

Strathern, Marilyn (1988) *The Gender of the Gift. Problems with Women and Problems with Society in Melanesia*. Berkeley, Calif.: University of California Press

—— (1992) *After Nature. English Kinship in the Late Twentieth Century*. Cambridge: Cambridge University Press

Tajfel, Henri (1978) *The Social Psychology of Minorities*. London: Minority Rights Group, report no. 38

Tambs-Lyche, Harald (1980) *London Patidars*. London: Routledge

Taylor, Anne-Christine (1991) 'Ethnie'. In Pierre Bonté and Michel Izard, eds., *Dictionnaire de l'ethnologie et de l'anthropologie*, pp. 242–4. Paris: Presses Universitaires Françaises

Taylor, John (1992) 'Touched with glory: heroes and human interest in the news'. In James Aulich, ed., *Framing the Falklands War. Nationhood, Culture and Identity*, pp. 13–32. Milton Keynes: Open University Press

Thaiss, Gustav (1978) 'The conceptualization of social change through metaphors'. *Journal of Asian and African Studies*, vol. 13 (1), pp. 1–13

Tinker, Hugh (1974) *A New Form of Slavery: The Export of Indian Labour Overseas 1880–1920*. Oxford: Oxford University Press

Todorov, Tzvetan (1989) *Nous et les autres. La réflexion française sur la diversité humaine*. Paris: Seuil

Tonkin, Elizabeth, Maryon McDonald and Malcolm Chapman, eds. (1989) *History and Ethnicity*. London: Routledge

Turner, Bryan S., ed. (1990) *Theories of Modernity and Postmodernity*. London: Sage

Turner, Victor (1967) *The Forest of Symbols*. Ithaca, NY.: Cornell University Press

—— (1969) *The Ritual Process: Structure and Anti-structure*. Chicago: Aldine

Van den Berghe, Pierre L. (1975) 'Ethnicity and class in highland Peru'. In Leo Despres, ed., *Ethnicity and Resource Competition in Plural Societies*, pp. 71–85. The Hague: Mouton

—— (1981) *The Ethnic Phenomenon*. New York: Elsevier Press

—— (1983) 'Class, race and ethnicity in Africa'. *Ethnic and Racial Studies*, vol. 6 (2), pp. 221–36

Vertovec, Steven (1991) 'Religion and ethnic ideology: the Hindu youth movement in Trinidad'. *Ethnic and Racial Studies*, vol. 13 (2), pp. 225–49

—— (1992) *Hindu Trinidad*. London: Macmillan

Wallerstein, Immanuel (1991a) 'Does India exist?' In Immanuel Wallerstein, *Unthinking Social Science: The Limits of Nineteenth-century Paradigms*, pp. 130–4. Cambridge: Polity

——— (1991b) *Unthinking Social Science: The Limits of Nineteenth-century Paradigms*. Cambridge: Polity

Wallman, Sandra (1986) 'Ethnicity and the boundary process in context'. In David Mason and John Rex, eds., *Theories of Race and Ethnic Relations*, pp. 226–35. Cambridge: Cambridge University Press

Wardhaugh, Ronald (1987) *Languages in Competition*. Oxford: Blackwell

Weber, Eugen (1976) *Peasants into Frenchmen: The Modernization of Rural France 1870–1914*. Stanford, Calif.: Stanford University Press

Williams, Brackette (1989) 'A class act: anthropology and the race to nation across ethnic terrain'. *Annual Review of Anthropology*, vol. 18, pp. 401–4

——— (1991) *Stains on My Name, War in My Veins: Guyana and the Politics of Cultural Struggle*. Durham: Duke University Press

Williams, Raymond (1976) *Keywords*. London: Flamingo

Willie, Charles V. (1991) 'Caste, class and family life chances'. In Rutledge M. Dennis, ed., *Research in Ethnic Relations*, vol. 6, pp. 65–84. London: JAI Press

Wilmsen, E.N. (1989) *Land Filled with Flies: A Political Economy of the Kalahari*. Chicago: University of Chicago Press

Wilson, Godfrey (1941–2) *An Essay on the Economics of Detribalization in Northern Rhodesia, Parts I–II*. Livingston: Rhodes-Livingstone Institute

Wilson, Peter J. (1978) *Crab Antics*, 2nd edition. New Haven, Conn.: Yale University Press

Wilson, William J. (1978) *The Declining Significance of Race*. Chicago: University of Chicago Press

Wirth, Louis (1956 [1928]) *The Ghetto*. Chicago: Chicago University Press

Wolf, Eric (1982) *Europe and the People without History*. Berkeley, Calif.: University of California Press

Worsley, Peter (1984) *The Three Worlds: Culture & World Development*. London: Weidenfeld & Nicholson

Yelvington, Kevin (1991) 'Ethnicity as practice? A comment on Bentley'. *Comparative Studies in Society and History*, vol. 33 (1), pp. 158–68

INDEX

Pluto Press
Anthropology, Culture and Society Series

Small Places, Big Issues

An Introduction to Social and Cultural Anthropology

Thomas Hylland Eriksen

The first introductory text to social and cultural
anthropology prepared for students of social sciences
at first year degree level.

Illustrated with black and white photographs.

Contents:

Thomas Hylland Eriksen is Senior Lecturer in Social
Anthropology at the University of Oslo

ISBN hardback 0 7453 0952 6; softback 0 7453 0951 8

Order from your local bookseller or contact the publisher on
081 348 2724.

Pluto Press

345 Archway Road, London N6 5AA
5500 Central Avenue, Boulder, Colorado 80301, USA

Pluto Press
Anthropology, Culture and Society Series

Women of a Lesser Cost

Female Labour, Foreign Exchange and Philippine
Development

Sylvia Chant and Cathy McIlwaine

This book explores one of the most important questions in
current research on gender and development – the links
among women's employment, migration and household
organisation.

Drawing on over 400 interviews with workers, households
and employers in the Philippine Visayas, Chant and
McIlwaine provide new insights for theories surrounding
women's work and its implications for gender roles and
relations.

The authors show that despite the embeddedness of
gender inequalities in all these spheres, Filipino women do
stand to gain some benefit from increased demand for their
labour.

Sylvia Chant is Lecturer in the Geography department at the
London School of Economics and is a specialist on gender
and development. **Cathy McIlwaine** is a Research Officer at
the London School of Economics.

ISBN hardback 0 7453 0946 1; softback 0 7453 0945 3

Order from your local bookseller or contact the publisher on
081 348 2724.

Pluto Press

345 Archway Road, London N6 5AA
5500 Central Avenue, Boulder, Colorado 80301, USA

Pluto Press
Anthropology, Culture and Society Series

Power and Its Disguises

Anthropological Perspectives on Politics

John Gledhill

Power and Its Disguises explores the differences between the experience and nature of power in different kinds of societies and presents a study of informal power relations, social movements and power in everyday life.

The book ends with a discussion of the political role of anthropology itself, a discipline born in colonialism which nevertheless confronts its largely middle-class practitioners with an uncomfortably close view of both the needs and struggles of individuals and communities facing injustice and oppression.

A controversial and thought provoking study.

John Gledhill teaches anthropology at University College London and is a specialist on contemporary rural society and politics in Latin America.

ISBN hardback 0 7453 0738 8; softback 0 7453 0739 6

Order from your local bookseller or contact the publisher on 081 348 2724.

Pluto Press

345 Archway Road, London N6 5AA
5500 Central Avenue, Boulder, Colorado 80301, USA